Reflections on the Common W… …ngs for Year C

Feeding on God's Word

SUSAN SAYERS

kevin mayhew

First published in 2003 by

KEVIN MAYHEW LTD
Buxhall, Stowmarket, Suffolk, IP14 3BW
E-mail: info@kevinmayhewltd.com

KINGSGATE PUBLISHING INC
1000 Pannell Street, Suite G, Columbia, MO 65201
E-mail: sales@kingsgatepublishing.com

These texts first appeared in *Living Stones – Complete Resource Book, Year C*

9 8 7 6 5 4 3 2 1 0

ISBN 1 84417 147 7
Catalogue No 1500642

Cover design by Jonathan Stroulger
Edited by Katherine Laidler

Printed and bound in Great Britain

Foreword

These reflections on the weekly readings are not new material – they come from the Complete Resource Book in the *Living Stones* programme, which follows the Common Worship Lectionary in the Anglican Church. Their publication in this separate book – here covering the readings for Year C – has been widely requested from various sources and for various reasons.

- Those who cannot get to church often, or who receive communion at home or in hospital, would like some help with reading the weekly Bible passages so they can be spiritually fed, and feel more part of the ongoing exploration of Scripture by the rest of the congregation.
- Discussion groups deciding to focus on the following week's readings express a need for the collected reflections in a separate book so that each group member can have a copy.
- Individuals wanting to prepare themselves for the worship Sunday by Sunday, or reflect on the previous week's readings, would like a book to help them. *Feeding on God's Word* serves this need.
- Those leading intercessions and reading the Bible passages during worship would value the reflections to help in their preparation.
- Those planning work with children and young people would like each team member to have a copy of the Scripture references and the reflection on those readings in order to feed them spiritually and better inform their prayer and preparation. Their own insights can then be incorporated in their ministry.

- Those with the talk or sermon to prepare would like their own copy of the Bible references and reflections to jump-start sermon preparation.

So, having heard all the requests, here is the book! I hope it will be useful to you all. These reflections don't pretend to be anything more than my own thinking as I read and pray the Scripture passages for each week. But I do believe that as more and more people in the church commit themselves to praying for God's guiding, reading the Bible sections for each Sunday, and reflecting on them with the help of a book like this, together with a good commentary where necessary, the whole people of God will be fed – properly fed in a deep and wholesome way.

We are called to be bread-sharers as Christians, and that includes both word and sacrament. As we share the meal of Scripture week by week, as well as the meal of bread and wine, we will be nourished and strengthened for the daily work of love to which God invites us.

SUSAN SAYERS

Contents

First Sunday of Advent

Thought for the day

The gathered hopes of generations remind us to get ourselves ready, so that Christ's return will be a day of excitement and great joy.

Reflection on the readings

Jeremiah 33:14-16; Psalm 25:1-10
1 Thessalonians 3:9-13; Luke 21:25-36

Today is filled with a sense of expectancy. It's rather like knowing that when you come of age you'll inherit a fortune, or that in another few years your TESSA account will mature. Only this is rather more mind-blowing than mere financial hope. The promise is there and stands secure, and God, being faithful, will keep that promise. Eventually, when the time is ripe, he will gather up all the goodness and honour and patience and long-suffering that has been grown throughout the ages, and bring things to completion.

This week's readings speak to the deep-seated longings of humanity for right and justice to triumph. They speak to our yearning for a final end to all the cruelty and misery of our world, some of which we all know from first-hand experience. Of course, it is serious and sombre stuff to be considering the winding-up of all the created universe as we know it, and it is very necessary to be reminded of our need to be ready by the lives we are leading.

Yet running through the readings is a clear, bright shaft of strong and exhilarating hope, which we can catch and make our own. God is familiar with our world. He too hears the cry, generation by generation, of those who find faith in a good God impossible because they are overwhelmed by the sorrows and tragedies screaming at them. But ultimately, as Christ has already shown us on the cross, and in his risen life, it is good that triumphs, and God's harvesting at the end of time will be a glorious celebration of all that is just, right and loving. This is not wishful thinking but hope, in all its integrity.

Second Sunday of Advent

Thought for the day

It had been prophesied that there would be a messenger to prepare the way for the coming of the Messiah. Now John the Baptist appears with his urgent message of repentance.

Reflection on the readings

Malachi 3:1-4; Canticle: Benedictus
Philippians 1:3-11; Luke 3:1-6

Today we read one example of many references from the prophets to a messenger who will prepare people for the coming of the anointed one, the long-awaited Messiah or Christ. It is typical of God's provision for his people. All teachers and builders know the necessity for thorough preparation and the way this so often involves chipping back to the solid foundations and making good. Anyone in advertising knows that people may need telling the same thing several times before they are likely to do anything about changing their favourite product.

So God, knowing human nature affectionately and realistically, tells us beforehand what he will do, and then provides John who himself points towards someone else. Hopefully there will be those who, having heard the prophecies, will already be waiting expectantly, ready to latch on to what the messenger is saying. There will be those who, through John's urgent message, will be sorting their lives out so that when Jesus' ministry begins, their hearts will already be attuned to receive what he has to say and eventually to recognise who he is.

And what about us? Paul's prayer, similar to that in the letter to the Thessalonians last week, is rather like the image of carrying a very full mug of tea from the kitchen back to bed, carefully holding it so that nothing spills and nothing is lost on the way. We are in the privileged position of having read the prophesies, seen them fulfilled in John the Baptist, and having met Jesus through the Gospels and his living presence. So in a sense we are like the full mug of tea. What we now have to do is make the journey to death and the second coming without losing a drop of what we have been given.

At another level is the recognition that it isn't enough to hear John's message once. It does us all good to use each Advent as a fresh chance to look at our lives and habits, and sort them out; to be ruthless about anything which is impairing our walk with God.

Third Sunday of Advent

Thought for the day

Our period of preparation shifts from repentance and forgiveness to the freed exhilaration of hope, as the momentous truth of God's immanence begins to dawn on us.

Reflection on the readings

Zephaniah 3:14-20; Canticle: Isaiah 12:2-6
Philippians 4:4-7; Luke 3:7-18

Over the first two weeks in Advent we have been focusing our attention on putting our lives straight, and this may well have been a very challenging and painful task. We may still be wrestling with its implications.

The shaft of hope has always been present in all this. But now it is as if the forgiveness we are receiving, resulting from real repentance, has enabled that shaft of hope to flood us with unexpected light and joy. From the viewpoint of forgiveness, the coming of Christ, both as we look back to Bethlehem and forward to the last day, is not something to fear, but to anticipate with great delight and enthusiasm.

There is Zephaniah's image of light-hearted and liberated singing and dancing, with something of the flavour of the street parties which celebrate peace after war. And there is Paul's signing-off message as he draws to a close his letter to the Christians at Philippi, the sense of God's closeness throbbing through the words. Everything is going to be all right; they can rejoice and go on rejoicing, whatever the immediate sufferings, because God has them ultimately safe.

And the people are enthusiastically taking up John the Baptist's challenge, and throwing themselves into giving up the behaviour they'd probably always known was wrong, but which they had never had the desire to address before.

In the gathering momentum some of them get over-enthusiastic, and how easily John could have been tempted to go along with their misguided assumptions.

Thankfully his own rigorous self-awareness keeps him humble, and he is able to use their questions to point their expectations in the right direction – towards the Christ.

Fourth Sunday of Advent

Thought for the day

When we co-operate with God amazing things happen.

Reflection on the readings

Micah 5:2-5a; Canticle: Magnificat or Psalm 80:1-7
Hebrews 10:5-10; Luke 1:39-45 (46-55)

It is not only Mary and Elizabeth who are pregnant in today's readings. The whole atmosphere this week is full of expectancy and the sense that what we are looking forward to has already begun to be fulfilled. It may be hidden but it leaps within us.

The prophet Micah speaks of events far greater than he imagines, and we, with our knowledge of the Gospel, can pick up on the image of a shepherd saviour being brought to birth and establishing a reign of peace. The writer of the letter to the Hebrews reminds us not just of Christ's birth but also of his death. As an unborn child already has the DNA pattern for the potential adult, so we are given here a kind of spiritual antenatal scan of Jesus, stretching back into the longing and forward to the sacrificial giving which secures our future.

There is enormous strength in the capacity to set aside something precious to you in order that a greater good may be enabled to happen. We marvel at Jesus laying aside his glory; laying aside his garments to wash the disciples' feet; laying aside the law – all in obedience and out of love. It is a hallmark of true Godliness.

So when we find human beings like Mary willing to lay aside so much in obedience and out of love, we are watching the most real and beautiful of human nature; God and humanity co-operating together for the good of the world.

Today we are given the chance to press the pause button as Mary and Elizabeth meet, with their unborn children within them, and wonder at what can happen when we allow God to work in us and with us for the good of the world.

Christmas Day

Thought for the day

Emmanuel – 'God with us' – is born at Bethlehem into the human family. Now we will be able to understand, in human terms, what God is really like.

Reflection on the readings

Isaiah 9:2-7
Psalm 96
Titus 2:11-14
Luke 2:1-14 (15-20)

The rejoicing Isaiah speaks of is a deliriously abandoned relief. After years and generations of oppression and injustice, this coming day is filled with evocative images of the security of a good harvest, the elation of overcoming an enemy in battle, and the freedom of slavery yokes being triumphantly shattered.

Typically, God brings about this longed-for day amid all the noise and confusion of ordinary life, with the census crowds jostling for space in the Bethlehem streets, the usual mix of noble and base behaviour, and in the context of unsettling circumstances. It is as if God is proving a point by acting out his name 'Emmanuel'; as if he is emphasising beyond doubt that he is truly with us in the untidy and muddled world we really inhabit. Nothing special is expected to be laid on, because he is not coming to meet us on our best behaviour, but on our real behaviour.

It is only when we are ourselves before God that he can truly be born in us. And if that place is crowded and dusty, or insecure or dark or full of questions, then he will be feeling very much at home.

First Sunday of Christmas

Thought for the day

Jesus' perception and understanding of his purpose and work begins to take shape throughout his childhood.

Reflection on the readings

1 Samuel 2:18-20, 26; Psalm 148
Colossians 3:12-17; Luke 2:41-52

It is significant that the young Samuel is clothed in the priestly ephod. Although Eli's sons are treating the Lord with contempt by their behaviour, this young child is innocent and clothed in a symbol of purity. In this climate of right living and integrity the child's family is blessed and Samuel himself grows in favour both with God and people.

The reading is linked with the passage from Colossians, where we are reminded of our calling to be Christians and the clothing that entails. It is a clothing with those qualities of good Christian living which are so often lacking in our world, and often dismissed or despised. Yet, as people sense things moving out of control, and the extent of violence and the breakdown of trust shock us into taking stock of our direction, there is also a yearning for the possibility of these qualities of compassion, kindness, humility, gentleness and patience. Samuel is a symbol of hope in any corrupt society.

As we celebrate the Incarnation it is important that we also have this picture of a gradually developing recognition in the child Jesus of his life's work and purpose. Like Samuel he knows he is set apart, and throughout his early childhood Mary, Joseph and Jesus must have talked together about the events surrounding his birth. Now, at the annual Passover visit to Jerusalem, with Jesus come of age in the Jewish tradition, he is starting to see the prophecies and hints of scripture adding up, and the vision of his role and purpose sharpens into focus.

Mary, scolding him in her anxiety for his safety, points out that she and his father have been worried sick, searching for him. Jesus, with the enormity of his life's work flooding into consciousness, has spent the past few days beginning to grasp what it means to be God's son, and cannot understand why they should be searching for him when he is at home in his Father's house. Capital letters are not always audible! No wonder Mary and Joseph couldn't understand what he was saying to them – they hadn't been part of this emerging revelation taking place in the temple.

It is rather comforting to read that Jesus went back to live according to their rules, nursing his vision as Mary nursed her experiences, treasuring them but not imposing them on anyone. Not even sharing them until the time was right. God will always go with us at our own pace and in ways that we can cope with. That is all part of what Incarnation means.

Second Sunday of Christmas

Thought for the day

Christ is the way God tells people about himself.

Reflection on the readings

Jeremiah 31:7-14
Psalm 147:12-20
Ephesians 1:3-14
John 1:(1-9) 10-18

Jeremiah lived his dream. He hated standing out against the rulers, priests and people, but because he knew it had to be done, he did it, and suffered imprisonment, torture, derision and rejection because of it. Yet through all this the great vision of hope shines clear, of a time when, with a new and direct relationship with God, the remnant will be restored and comforted, led by a good shepherd. Rather like Jesus, Jeremiah's message was as much his life as his words.

In the letter to the Ephesians, Paul takes up Jeremiah's prophecy and sees it fulfilled in the community of the followers of Christ. Through Christ we can have this new and direct relationship with God, and so receive the grace which makes forgiveness and a new start possible.

John's introduction to his Gospel draws all this together, as he speaks of Christ as the Word – the Message – of God, always present and part of him, and proclaiming God clearly, as a living Message, as he walked about on earth. Today we are given total cinema, so to speak; we are looking at the past, present and future all at once so that God's purpose, and its fulfilment, are seen together. That is the extraordinary truth of the Incarnation: God was, God is, and God will be. And we can see it in the person of Jesus.

The Epiphany

Thought for the day

Jesus, the hope of the nations, is shown to the world.

Reflection on the readings

Isaiah 60:1-6
Psalm 72:(1-9) 10-15
Ephesians 3:1-12
Matthew 2:1-12

Beginning with one person (Abraham) and developing to embrace one family and eventually one nation, God has painstakingly planted the seed of salvation and nurtured it until the whole earth is involved. Isaiah had sensed that day in terms of a sunrise dawning with the light of day on a world of darkness, with all the hope and joy and relief that a new day can bring after a long, dark night. Probably this was one of the prophecies these magi had read as they studied the signs of the sky and wondered about life's meaning. And perhaps it was then that they felt stirring in them a profound calling to be, in person, those visitors who could symbolise the light dawning on the wider world. Certainly they must have been inspired by a powerful sense of urgency and necessity to make such a journey. And as they travelled, both physically and spiritually, towards Bethlehem, bearing the gifts laid down in those ancient scriptures, perhaps they were drawn by much more than a star. Jesus later proclaimed that anyone who sets out to search always finds.

Paul also knows himself to be commissioned to explain God's nature to the Gentiles. He is overwhelmed by the extraordinary way that the Christ has enabled us to approach the great and awesome God with freedom and confidence – as one of the family. And for all of us who are Gentiles, the feast of the Epiphany is particularly one to celebrate, since it marks the truth that we too are part of God's salvation and can share the light of dawn.

The Baptism of Christ: First Sunday of Epiphany

Thought for the day

Jesus is baptised, and God confirms his identity and his calling.

Reflection on the readings

Isaiah 43:1-7
Psalm 29
Acts 8:14-17
Luke 3:15-17, 21-22

Choosing names for our children is an important job, and one which most family members are more than happy to help with! Using one another's names in conversation is an important way of emphasising our concern for one another as precious and unique. To lovers the name of the beloved is deeply emotive. To be known by name indicates a closeness of relationship which as humans we value. It was hearing her name spoken that made Mary Magdalene realise she was in the presence of the risen Jesus.

As the Isaiah passage reminds us, God has called each of us by name; he knows and loves us as individuals, with our own particular mix of gifts and problems. The redemption he brings is personal and answers our particular deepest needs. It is good to celebrate this on the day we remember the Baptism of Christ, since each person's Baptism is not only their decision to commit themselves to Christ, but also God's calling to each by name.

We are told that at Jesus' Baptism the Holy Spirit

descended on him in bodily form like a dove, as he stood praying. God was confirming Jesus' identity as his Son, with whom he was well pleased, and affirming his calling as Saviour of the world.

Second Sunday of Epiphany

Thought for the day

As a marriage celebrates the beginning of a changed, new life for the bride and groom, so our loving, faithful God has chosen us and is ready to transform our lives for the good of the world.

Reflection on the readings

Isaiah 62:1-5; Psalm 36:5-10
1 Corinthians 12:1-11; John 2:1-11

Today the nature of our relationship with God is expressed in terms of marriage. Starting with our experience of the best in human love, we can use this to imagine the totally loving, totally faithful nature of our God. Really, of course, it is the other way round: being made in the likeness of God we share, in part, his capacity for faithfulness and loving which is often expressed in the decision to marry the object of our deep love and affection.

At a marriage celebration there is in many cultures a symbolic change of name, to signify that there has been a fundamental life change and that the two are now one. In a similar way God first loves us and chooses us, and then calls us onwards into so changed a life in him that it is often referred to as being born again into a new life.

The passage from 1 Corinthians explores how this new life in the Spirit manifests itself. Paul is anxious to make it clear that there is no rigid format for our new life. It is as varied and diverse as we are, reflecting all the richness of individual gifts. But for all the differences there is a bond of unity, because all these gifts are expressions of the one Spirit. We can get ourselves unnecessarily worked up about the distribution of such gifts. If, instead, we keep our eyes on Jesus, the gifts can be received and valued wherever and however they happen to show up.

The transformation of our lives could not be shown more dramatically than in the Gospel event of the water being transformed into wine at the marriage in Cana. The ordinary is turned into the remarkable through contact with and obedience to the word, or Word, of God.

Third Sunday of Epiphany

Thought for the day

The meaning of the scriptures
is revealed to the people.

Reflection on the readings

Nehemiah 8:1-3, 5-6, 8-10; Psalm 19
1 Corinthians 12:12-31a; Luke 4:14-21

Sometimes we may be reading a very familiar passage of scripture, yet for the first time it seems to shoot out at us with great significance and we realise with a shock that it is exactly what we needed to hear. When this happens it reminds us of the way the scriptures are much more than historical data and fine literature. They are also in-breathed with God's presence so that through them we can be given God's guidance.

As the law was read out to that ancient crowd in the square in front of the temple, we can imagine their emotions: sorrow and grief as it suddenly dawned on them how they had neglected their spiritual heritage, the yearning to put things right, and the joy that at last they were able to see things more clearly. It seems to be a hallmark of God's way of doing things that instead of condemnation, he gently brings us to see for ourselves what and where we are wrong, and gives with this insight a joy and excitement at the prospect of putting things right.

In the Gospel we see another congregation, gathered and attentive as the scriptures are read. But there is a difference, which Jesus must have been aware of even before he started his teaching. These people were his own people, the people he had grown up with, representative of the chosen people of Israel. They are privileged to be hearing the scriptures explained by the Word of God in person. And yet whether or not they were able to receive him and what he said would depend on where they were spiritually as they sat there that morning. Jesus cannot but reveal to us the truth, because that is his nature. If we are to recognise it as the truth, we need to make sure we are open and receptive.

The Church is a body of people, rich from its diversity of types and gifts, and strong when it recognises its unity in Christ. When as a body we are open and receptive, the life of Christ in us can speak out love and truth to the world. But wherever individual members lose their receptiveness to Christ, the whole body is seriously weakened.

Fourth Sunday of Epiphany

Thought for the day

At eight days old, Jesus is presented in the temple, and at the Purification is revealed to Simeon and Anna as the promised Saviour who is able to reveal to us our true selves.

Reflection on the readings

Ezekiel 43:27-44:4; Psalm 48
1 Corinthians 13:1-13; Luke 2:22-40

This week is the last in the series of 'showings', or Epiphany. Simeon and Anna are wonderful examples of the elderly faithful who have stayed spiritually flexible and alert throughout their long lives. Simeon has been told by God that he will see the Messiah in person before he dies, and we can imagine his excitement as on this particular day he feels drawn to go to the temple court. His trust in God is such that he will not be thrown by anything unexpected, and as soon as he sees this unremarkable little family walking in with their new baby he knows beyond all doubt that this is the child he has been waiting all his life to see.

As the wise men were in a sense representative of all Gentiles, so Simeon and Anna are representative of the faithful remnant of Israel, watching and waiting with Godly living and a hopeful heart. Typically, God nudges them to be there at exactly the right time to witness God's Son being presented in God's dwelling-place, the temple.

Ezekiel's vision of a guided tour around the temple reminds the people in exile of their glorious heritage, and it is interesting to have this particular passage today. We are bound to pick up echoes of only the prince being allowed to enter by the holy gate, as we hear of Jesus being carried in and recognised by those who are wise and mature in the Spirit. God's glory is expressed both in the awesome beauty of holiness and in the immanent vulnerability of a human baby.

Simeon has no problem with Jesus being the light for the whole world because he has never allowed legalism to hide or quench the flame of truth. But this perception also enables him to see something of the inevitable 'suffering servant' role the Messiah will have as he reveals people to themselves. Some will find this the key to new life, while others will prefer to reject the light of truth. Simeon can see that an intrinsic part of saving through love and truth is making enemies and meeting conflict and suffering; suffering that this young woman, his mother, is bound to share.

The beautiful and familiar Corinthians passage in praise of love speaks of Godly love that has no limit, the kind of love exemplified in the life of Jesus. The closer we stay to Jesus, the more loving we shall become ourselves, and the more our potential selves we will become.

Proper 1

Sunday between 3 and 9 February inclusive
(if earlier than the Second Sunday before Lent)

Thought for the day

God calls his people and commissions them.

Reflection on the readings

Isaiah 6:1-8 (9-13); Psalm 138
1 Corinthians 15:1-11; Luke 5:1-11

We can be driving along the motorway without a care in the world until we glance at the petrol gauge and discover that we are about to run out of fuel. Suddenly we are anxiously watching the miles to the next service station, and at the first opportunity we drive in with great relief to sort things out. Similarly, it is only when we suddenly catch sight of God that the meanness of our lives sharpens into focus and we cannot wait to put things right. Before we noticed, we were quite happy to carry on as we were.

It is when Isaiah sees that vision of God in glory that he is suddenly aware of the lack of righteousness and integrity both in his own life and his society. It is when Simon sees the signs of God's power in the catch of fish that he feels completely unworthy to be in the company of Jesus.

At this point it is always God's nature to reach out and never to condemn. Isaiah has his guilt taken away by the angel's burning coal from the altar, and Jesus rescues Simon, telling him not to be afraid. Our God is full of compassion and mercy, and will never take advantage of us at moments of weakness or vulnerability. The realisation is necessary for restoration to happen but, the moment we see the problem, God helps and enables us to put things right.

Only after this does God commission us, involving us and working with our consent each step of the way. All three characters in our readings today – Isaiah, Paul and Simon – have been made so acutely aware of the need that they enthusiastically agree to work with God. I love this characteristic of God's; the way he almost gets us thinking his commission is our idea! Sometimes after prayer about something we will get a sudden and unexpected good idea which we can't wait to put into practice. It may well be that God was speaking silently into our hearts.

As a result of God's commissioning, the good news is spread. Those who have recently had their eyes opened are still excited by what they can see, and their excitement is infectious, so they are particularly effective at spreading the news.

Proper 2

Sunday between 10 and 16 February inclusive
(if earlier than the Second Sunday before Lent)

Thought for the day

The challenges and rewards of living by faith.

Reflection on the readings

Jeremiah 17:5-10; Psalm 1
1 Corinthians 15:12-20; Luke 6:17-26

It is always noticeable how much less you spend if for some reason you can't get out. Shops rely on our habit of browsing and getting what we don't particularly need. Several times an hour on radio and television we are persuaded to invest in all those things we cannot possibly live without, and the social pressure to wear or use or play with particular brand-name items is very strong. The young, and the insecure, are particularly vulnerable.

Such consumerism is a symptom of our trust in things and systems and wealth and power. We bank on all this bringing us happiness and fulfilment. And although the actual items change across the centuries, the basic problem is exactly the same now as it was in the days of Jeremiah. Through him God spoke to his people of the foolishness of living with our faith in things which cannot ever satisfy and which stunt our spiritual growth.

The lovely image of a strongly rooted tree near the water, so that its leaves are always green, shows up the blessings to the whole community, as well as the individual, that spring from right living, based on trust in God. Psalm 1 also reflects on this valuable fruitfulness of well-rooted lives.

Jesus' teaching in today's Gospel comes after the resentful anger of the teachers and Pharisees resulting from his healing on the Sabbath, and after the apostles have been chosen and called. Luke sets the beatitudes on a level place with a large crowd, and Jesus is looking at his disciples as he speaks. We can only guess at what was going through the minds of these people. They have given up their security and their earning potential, they have no idea where their next meal will be coming from, and they have glimpsed the hostility they are inviting by committing themselves to walking around with this leader.

Jesus speaks into their possible misgivings and natural concerns, reassuring them that although they have chosen poverty, insecurity, insult and rejection, they have indeed chosen wisely and bravely, and the rewards of living by faith are great and lasting. In contrast, those who cling to the material, intellectual or even religious security, which stunts their growth and anchors them to the ground, can never be swept up in the wind of the spirit and experience the fullness of joy God longs to provide.

The quantity of our possessions does need looking at, and we cannot sweep such teaching comfortably into the realm of attitudes towards our wealth and lifestyle. If we are really living by faith in God it is bound to affect our comfort. If we know we have given up anything or any relationship for the sake of living God's way, then today's Gospel is reassuring and comforting us that we have chosen well and in the long term the tears will be wiped away.

And if we discover that much of our happiness is linked with things, or systems, or others' praise, then today's readings challenge us to choose the risky vulnerability of living instead by faith in God.

Proper 3

Sunday between 17 and 23 February inclusive
(if earlier than the Second Sunday before Lent)

Thought for the day

Jesus teaches us to love our enemies
and forgive those who sin against us.

Reflection on the readings

Genesis 45:3-11, 15; Psalm 37:1-11, 39-40
1 Corinthians 15:35-38, 42-50; Luke 6:27-38

The last time the brothers had seen Joseph they had just sold him to some traders and they were about to tell their father that Joseph had been killed by wild animals. No wonder they are afraid when Joseph turns up in this position of power and authority. Surely he is bound to want revenge? But no. Instead we find him overjoyed to see his brothers again, and able to recognise the good that has come from a terrible situation. There is no bitterness or harboured resentment, and it is a mark of Joseph's closeness to God that he is able to behave like this.

So often we insist on carrying grudges, and they weigh us down. They imprison us and prevent us from knowing inner peace. In advising us to forgive those who sin against us, and to love our enemies, Jesus is actually setting us free from the chains we clank around with us, sometimes for years.

Jesus would not have been talking simply to a group of friends and sympathisers at this point. Among his hearers there were no doubt some who regarded Jesus as their enemy, so this teaching was very close to the bone. While your heart is filled with hurt and anger and hatred towards someone, the last thing you want to do is love and forgive them. It can be a real battleground as we wrestle with our rage and disappointment and frustration, and it is important that we don't pretend these feelings are not there. To squash such emotions deep down inside us and sit on them is in no way forgiveness. Yet neither are these very real emotions an excuse for permitting us to behave badly.

We do need to recognise and acknowledge them, asking for God's grace to transform what is going on inside us, and then face the battle which may be long and difficult. But if we really want God's will to be done in us then we are playing on the winning side, and victory over revenge, resentment and hatred will eventually come. That victory is a cleansing and wonderfully refreshing desire to forgive. And it melts the hatred away.

Second Sunday before Lent

Thought for the day

'He commands even the winds and the water and they obey him.'

Reflection on the readings

Genesis 2:4b-9, 15-25; Psalm 65
Revelation 4; Luke 8:22-25

As humans we are naturally curious about who we are and where we came from. We first wonder about these things when we are toddlers and are still thinking about it a lifetime later. Today's creation story is the older and more primitive of the two in Genesis. What truth does it proclaim? How does it help us in our understanding of the human story?

We find here that God is in charge, and his provision is both complete and flexible. He moulds the man and other creatures from mud, starts a garden, and operates on the man so that both he and the woman are of the same material; they are one flesh. There is a sense of a child creating a world in a sandpit – with all that care and overall vision deciding where things should be and how they should be done. There is close, practical involvement and good communication. God and humankind are working together. There is the energy of youth and the wisdom of age. So in this ancient story we can sense the truth of God's power, authority and sheer goodness, together with his intimacy with the humans he creates.

When we are living in harmony with the God who created us, there is indeed an inner peace which not even the best relaxation CDs can imitate, nor the best whisky provide. It comes free and holds us firm through the turbulence of a lifetime and beyond.

It is interesting that when the disciples in the storm wake Jesus in their terror of the life-threatening wind and water, he first calms the storm and then challenges their own inner storm of panic. 'Where is your faith?' he asks. We no doubt sympathise with the disciples here! Surely we are allowed a bit of panic at such times? But Jesus is drawing them to such a deep, secure knowledge of God's protective indwelling that they don't need to lose it completely even when threatened with death. If we think of the radiance of Stephen as he was stoned, for instance, we can see how such faith transforms our reaction to any disaster.

What the disciples began to understand through this experience in the boat, was the link between this extra-ordinary friend and teacher they had discovered, and the God of all creation.

Sunday before Lent

Thought for the day

God's glory makes Moses' face radiant,
and it transfigures Jesus as he prays on the mountain.
Our lives, too, can become increasingly radiant
as the Spirit transforms us.

Reflection on the readings

Exodus 34:29-35; Psalm 99
2 Corinthians 3:12-4:2; Luke 9:28-36 (37-43)

Those who are not committed Christians will often express disappointment at the selfish or immoral behaviour of churchgoing Christians. They obviously expect that our faith should make a big difference to the way we look, think and behave. I find this quite encouraging. Obviously it needs to be recognised that the Church is a 'school for sinners' and for those who know their need of God, rather than for the perfect. But it also suggests that those who make such remarks hang on to a belief in God's transforming power. And they are right to, because God can and does transform his close followers.

Moses, communing as a friend with God, comes away from the meetings with his face radiant and wears a veil to cover it. The veil prevents the people from seeing the glory of God which terrifies them, and Paul sees this as a foreshadowing of the way the people cannot or will not discern the glory of God revealed in Jesus. When we recognise Jesus it is as if the veil is finally lifted, and as we draw closer to God in this new relationship, the Spirit can begin to transform us until our lives begin to shine.

So why don't they? Sometimes they do and we don't notice. It is quite likely that if you told someone you had seen God's love in the way they behaved they would be surprised. It may be that people have seen his radiance in you on occasions. You cannot spend your time regularly in God's company and work at living his way without it changing you and making you beautiful. But we also have to recognise that half measures are not good enough, Jesus always presents us with this challenge: 'Who do you say that I am?' What we reply has a lot to do with recognising the glory shown in the Transfiguration, and that will affect how we decide to spend our time and money and choices.

First Sunday of Lent

Thought for the day

Following his baptism, Jesus is severely tempted out in the desert, and shows us how to overcome temptation.

Reflection on the readings

Deuteronomy 26:1-11; Psalm 91:1-2, 9-16
Romans 10:8b-13; Luke 4:1-13

We often use temptation as an excuse for sin. It is Satan's whispered lie that when temptation gets too strong we have no hope of resisting and can somehow plead diminished responsibility. So it is quite an eye-opener to watch Jesus in action. After all, the temptations are exceedingly powerful, and the stakes are so high. If the powers of darkness can sabotage God's plan of salvation almost before it has started, then humankind will be gloriously and utterly lost and God will have failed. Arrogance, as well as deceit, is a hallmark of Satan.

So how does Jesus deal with these temptations, and what can we learn from him to help us when we too are severely tempted?

One thing Jesus doesn't do is enter into an argument with Satan. He would lose, because temptations are always cleverly constructed and entirely logical, with enough truth in them to make them appear plausible. What Jesus does is to recognise the motive under the scheming and address this instead, reaching into the secure promises of God and holding firmly on to these.

Using the vulnerability of Jesus' hunger, Satan subtly grafts this on to a challenge to his role and authority so that we can barely see the join. Jesus refuses to get drawn into this, and recognises that the fast is making him vulnerable, so he encourages himself with God's words which affirm what he is doing and its value. In the next temptation Satan attempts to take Jesus' pondering over his mission and his urgent longing for the coming of the kingdom, and to distort this into the need for a quick and immediate answer, which Satan offers to provide. Jesus recognises Satan's apparent generosity for what it is, and reaches into the firm law of God to deliver another simple one-liner: We are to worship only God. End of story, end of negotiation.

In the final temptation, where Satan again homes in on Jesus' longing to draw people to recognise God at work among them, the longing is manipulated into the possibility of bypassing the expensive and time-consuming method of salvation by love. Discerning that Satan's 'helpful' suggestions are really about denying God's sovereignty and total righteousness, Jesus reminds himself as well as Satan of the command not to put God to the test.

All too often we let ourselves get drawn into Satan's arguments. Think of those times your conscience will whisper that you shouldn't be doing what you are, and all the justifications pour into your mind. If we take Jesus' example, we will refuse to listen to these plausible arguments, and reach instead for the deep truths we know of God, recognising that Satan will use our vulnerable areas, and try to distort our noble ones. If we stick firmly with the truths of God, they will reassure and affirm us enough to resist temptation. Contrary to what Satan tells us, temptation can be resisted and overcome.

Second Sunday of Lent

Thought for the day

If only we will agree to put our faith in God, he will fill our lives with meaning and bring us safely to heaven.

Reflection on the readings

Genesis 15:1-12, 17-18; Psalm 27
Philippians 3:17-4:1; Luke 13:31-35

On those occasions when you know the answer on a TV quiz programme and those on the panel don't, it's quite likely that you will be calling the answer out to them. The frustrating thing is that of course they insist on taking no notice of you, oblivious to your offers of help!

I sometimes wonder if God must feel the same frustration with us when we so often live oblivious to his offer of help and guidance. Not exactly like the TV panel, who actually cannot hear, even if they want to, but more like parents who must watch their child getting deeper involved in an unhealthy relationship which they know will end in misery, while their misgivings are dismissed as nagging, or simply ignored.

Jesus had so often longed to gather up the people of Jerusalem as a hen gathers her chickens to safety under her wings, but there is no way he will force his love and help on anyone, and if people refuse to come, he will always let them go the way they choose.

Yet the benefits from putting our faith in God are so remarkable. Today we see Abram believing God's promise in spite of its unlikeliness, and experiencing the power and greatness of God as the covenant is ratified. Psalm 27 is full of hope despite difficult circumstances because of the psalmist's trust in the faithful God. Such faith anchors us. It roots us so deeply that we are able to open up and live vulnerably. It enables us to stand firm through all circumstances and be less thrown by whatever life flings at us.

Third Sunday of Lent

Thought for the day

We have God's invitation to come and drink freely of his Spirit, but if we keep refusing his offer it will eventually be withdrawn.

Reflection on the readings

Isaiah 55:1-9; Psalm 63:1-8
1 Corinthians 10:1-13; Luke 13:1-9

When we are seriously thirsty we are no longer bothered about the choice of drink, but simply desperate for water. In extreme thirst the body shrieks for water, and a nomadic desert people would be well used to the power of such thirst. So the image of 'spiritual water' is a strong one, drawing on our life-and-death human need which is both physical and spiritual.

The invitation is not confined to the material or spiritually rich; it is freely available to everyone. Instead of wasting our time and money on poor-value substitutes we might as well go for the real thing: God himself.

So far it is all good news. But there is also a serious shadow which we have to address. God is no fool. He is wise to all our excuses for rejecting his offer. For all kinds of reasons we continue to invest in values and lifestyles and spending and habits which sell us short and bankrupt us spiritually. Sometimes we half convince ourselves that God doesn't notice, or even doesn't mind; that his understanding of why we do the things we do is so tolerant and accepting that we can mostly live as we like, especially if we are being 'true to ourselves'.

In today's reading Jesus is at pains to point out the dangers of living and thinking in this way. Of course it matters. Of course God knows exactly what we are doing and how we are living. And if we go on and on refusing to accept him on his terms, the truth must be faced that his invitation can be withdrawn.

Lent is an excellent time to look carefully at what our real response to him is, and act on what we see.

Fourth Sunday of Lent: Mothering Sunday

Thought for the day

While we are here in this life, given one another to care for, we can learn the lessons of mutual love and support and shared suffering.

Reflection on the readings

Exodus 2:1-10 or 1 Samuel 1:20-28
Psalm 34:11-20 or Psalm 127:1-4
2 Corinthians 1:3-7 or Colossians 3:12-17
Luke 2:33-35 or John 19:25-27

Both Moses and Samuel were marked and chosen to be spokesmen for God, and today we see the love their mothers have for them; love that extends to the letting go, but is in no way an abandoning or cutting-off.

And in the Gospel we see another side of motherhood, just as real and recognisable. It is the path of shared suffering which all parents will relate to. However old we and they get, our mothers still suffer our hurts with us. Pain that hurts us hurts them too. Simeon could see this shadow in Mary's future, and in John's Gospel we glimpse that tender reversal of roles that happens to many of us as we age, and find that, instead of caring for our children, they have started to take care of us. Jesus shows such loving care as he gives Mary and John one another to love and look after.

One of the greatest gifts God gives us in this life is one another. Together we walk through the years, learning to listen and scold, to encourage and forgive; learning to give and accept, to protect and let go; learning the responsibility of helping those dependent on us and the humility of enforced and unwelcome dependence on others.

And through all of it God gives the companionship and the joy of humans loving one another. There is a place for mothering in all relationships, including, of course, God's relationship with us.

Fifth Sunday of Lent

Thought for the day

When we are privileged to share in Christ's suffering,
we also share in his new life.

Reflection on the readings

Isaiah 43:16-21
Psalm 126
Philippians 3:4b-14
John 12:1-8

Today we become aware of the shadow of the cross as we draw closer to Holy Week and Easter. There is a sense of the inevitable sadness and suffering approaching as we sit with Jesus and his friends, and Mary anoints his feet with the pure nard as if lovingly and lavishly preparing him for death.

Yet, although there is sadness, this is not a time of despair or hopeless resignation. Far from it. Even as Judas dismisses Mary's act as sentimental extravagance, we know that this suffering will be the gateway to something of vital importance. The echoed words of the prophet – 'forget the former things – I am doing a new thing' – bring with them a wonder and excitement for the gathering momentum of Jesus' time on earth.

This is to be greater even than the great escape story of Exodus. This rescue will be God acting in an extraordinary way, breaking completely new ground.

Paul, writing to the Christians at Philippi, gives us such a catalogue of sufferings as to make anyone considering following Christ think again. Why commit yourself to something which will lead you into such discomfort and insult? Yet Paul sounds anything but resentful. He is so impressed by what he has gained in Christ that he's more than happy with the hardships. This suffering is positive and full of hope.

Palm Sunday

Thought for the day

As Jesus rides into Jerusalem on a donkey, and the crowds welcome him, we sense both the joy at the Messiah being acclaimed, and the heaviness of his suffering which follows. Jesus' mission is drawing to its fulfilment.

Reflection on the readings

Liturgy of the Palms:
Luke 19:28-40; Psalm 118:1-2, 19-29

Liturgy of the Passion:
Isaiah 50:4-9a; Psalm 31:9-16
Philippians 2:5-11; Luke 22:14-23:56 or Luke 23:1-49

It is no accident that the Isaiah reading, the Psalm and the passage from Philippians prepare us to hear the Gospel narrative of the Passion with our hearts as well as our ears. They have been chosen to work on our understanding and bring us to the point where we sense deep truths and echoes of hope, right in the centre of the gruelling and disturbing events of the Crucifixion. And even before these readings we will have joined with the crowds of Jerusalem in waving our palm branches and celebrating Jesus' entry into the city. It is a day of mood changes and can feel quite emotionally draining.

The Isaiah passage introduces us to the concept of the Saviour being a vulnerable, suffering servant, obedient to God's will, and utterly faithful to his calling, in spite of the rejection he receives and the way his mission is misinterpreted. Then the Psalm expresses firm trust in God's loving goodness which continues for ever. This is not a shallow feel-good factor, but a steady pulse of assurance which works in the bewildering and distressing times, as well as the times of relief and lighthearted happiness.

The letter to the Philippians focuses our attention on the amazingly generous nature of Christ's humility. With the Isaiah passage fresh in our minds, we realise that Jesus is taking on that suffering obedience of the loyal servant which is bound to bring with it rejection and worldly failure and misunderstanding.

So when we come to the story of the Passion in today's Gospel, all the echoes from Isaiah, the Psalm and Philippians are there, enabling us to grasp something of the cosmic proportions of what we are witnessing; something of the extraordinary love and provision, gracious humility and total faithfulness of our God.

Easter Day

Thought for the day

It is true. Jesus is alive for all time.
The Lord of life cannot be held by death.
God's victory over sin and death means that
new life for us is a reality.

Reflection on the readings

Acts 10:34-43 or Isaiah 65:17-25
Psalm 118:1-2, 14-24
1 Corinthians 15:19-26 or Acts 10:34-43
John 20:1-18 or Luke 24:1-12

Throughout the whole world today Christians are celebrating the most extraordinary event. Death, the most final thing we know as humans, has been the setting for the greatest regeneration story of all time. Jesus of Nazareth, handed over to the Roman authorities for execution and a cursed death, has been raised to a kind of life never before experienced. He has a body, the scars are still visible, he talks, listens and eats. Yet he is no longer bound by space or time.

In Christ's risen nature we sense the stirring of that new life described by Isaiah, freed from all the tragedy and pain of mortal life, and full of hope, joy and overwhelming fulfilment. But the Resurrection stories are about people who are emotionally confused and drained. The exhausting events of the past week have them seeing but not recognising, wondering and agonising but not immediately able to make sense of anything. And that is so human and reassuring for us to read.

So often it takes us years of living before we eventually grasp something of God's involvement in our journey or our pain. So often the evidence of his real, loving presence is staring us in the face, and yet we assume any number of other factors are responsible, much as Mary assumed Jesus was the gardener. And Peter was wallowing so deeply in his own misery and pessimism that he probably wouldn't have noticed Jesus if he had been standing there next to him. It may well have been that Jesus was!

With great gentleness and courtesy Jesus holds back on revealing the full power and vibrancy of his new life, so as to lead people at their own pace to recognise the astounding truth. He lets them see only what they are capable of assimilating, for he loves them, and has no desire to scare or overwhelm. That is just as true for us today. The more we seek this risen Lord, the more of him we will notice, recognise and delight in.

Second Sunday of Easter

Thought for the day

Having seen Jesus in person, the disciples are convinced of the Resurrection. We too can meet him personally.

Reflection on the readings

Acts 5:27-32; Psalm 118:14-29 or Psalm 150
Revelation 1:4-8; John 20:19-31

People will often say, 'If I hadn't seen it with my own eyes I'd never have believed it!' Sight is the sense we trust most for evidence and proof. There are many who assume God does not exist because they cannot see him with their eyes, and it is interesting that God has chosen to withhold from us that very proof of existence that we prize most highly. It's almost as if he is challenging us to be less dependent on this sense because our very mastery in sight can blind us to other kinds of perception.

The disciples had the women's eye-witness account to trust, but they didn't trust it. They were only convinced of the Resurrection when Jesus suddenly appeared right there in the room with them, talking with them and fully alive. We may think we are convinced of the Resurrection, but supposing the risen Christ suddenly appeared visually in the middle of our worship, and spoke to you, and looked you straight in the eye. I suspect our conviction would suddenly rocket, and we would be bursting to tell everyone about it.

In the reading from Acts we find the apostles doing just that, and getting themselves into a lot of trouble as a result. They argue that they cannot possibly stop teaching people about the risen Jesus because it's too important to keep quiet about. They are not saying, 'Some people believe that . . .' but 'We know this is true because we have actually witnessed it'.

The really exciting thing is that we can also meet the living Jesus personally. We may not be able to see him visually, but there is no doubt that he is with us in person whenever we gather to pray, whenever we share the bread and wine at Communion, and whenever we 'wash one another's feet' in loving service. Sometimes his presence is full of peace, sometimes reassuring, challenging or affirming, and as we become more attuned to his company, we come to realise that sight isn't the most important proof after all.

Third Sunday of Easter

Thought for the day

Those who know Jesus and recognise that he is the anointed Saviour are commissioned to go out as his witnesses to proclaim the good news.

Reflection on the readings

Acts 9:1-6 (7-20); Psalm 30
Revelation 5:11-14; John 21:1-19

This week the readings invite us to see the consequences of the Resurrection both from a heavenly and an earthly point of view at once, which is a very three-dimensional experience! In the passage from Revelation we see through the eyes of the visionary the ecstatic and eternal welcome given by the inhabitants of heaven to the triumphant Lamb of God, who has proved worthy of all honour, glory and praise through his total sacrifice, self-expending and loving obedience.

From the earthly point of view we have the disciples, so wonderfully human and well-meaning and bumbling, going back to the safe place they came from as a natural reaction to the trauma and turmoil of the present. We recognise the symptoms, as we remember our own tendency to settle into old established behaviour patterns if God's new direction for us is proving too challenging or too open-ended.

So, typically, our God makes his appearance in a place we will be bound to meet him: the place we are fishing in. As Jesus sets up his camp breakfast on the beach, he gives those friends he loves so fondly the opportunity to discover him, recognise him, and recommit themselves to his way of living. Gently and deliberately Jesus leads Peter to undo those denials and face the dangerous consequences of commitment realistically. There is a maturity about Peter's commitment now which is quite different from his previous enthusiastic claim that he would never forsake his Master. This commitment is quieter, and made with more self-knowledge. Peter is growing up.

Saul, too, receives his commission, and the fiery zeal of his desire to cleanse the Jewish faith of these dangerous heretics crumples in the shining light of Jesus' heavenly presence that he experiences on the Damascus road. Once again, Jesus has made his appearance where Saul has chosen to ride.

Whenever Jesus meets us and challenges us, we become his witnesses and are drawn into a commission which carries great responsibility. Those who have not met Jesus will judge him by the way we behave and speak.

Fourth Sunday of Easter

Thought for the day

Asked if he really is the Christ, Jesus directs his questioners to look at his life in action and see for themselves that he and the Father are one.

Reflection on the readings

Acts 9:36-43; Psalm 23
Revelation 7:9-17; John 10:22-30

With the benefit of hindsight we might wonder how people could fail to make the connection between Jesus' way of living and the promise of the Messiah. Surely for anyone fortunate enough to witness the miracles of healing, the teaching and the grace and wisdom of this man, the truth must have been obvious?

But in fact we often fail to notice the obvious, often because what we see is not what we were expecting, and our preconceived ideas can be most effective at blinding us for a while. We must also bear in mind the enormity of the implications for those who met him of Jesus being the Christ. It was vital that such a claim should be very thoroughly checked out and no rash decisions made. Jesus respects where we are all coming from, and his sensible advice to study the facts is a recognition, both of our need to make sound judgement and of the value of using the minds God has given us.

So, if we take Jesus' advice to his questioners and look at the signs and miracles, what do we see? We find deep compassion and love for people. We find the power of forgiveness being used to liberate imprisoned souls from guilt which has weighed them down for years. We even find the authority which can reach into death and pull people out. And, when we look at Jesus' followers, continuing his work in the power of the Spirit after the Resurrection, we see those same powers at work. Peter's approach to Tabitha has close connections with Jesus' raising of Jairus' daughter. Peter is clearly allowing the living Jesus to work through his own body in order to restore this woman to life. It is exactly the same power as we saw in Jesus' own physical ministry on earth.

The evidence points us in the direction of recognising, in the person of Jesus, the Christ or promised Messiah, at one with God the Father, and willing to rescue us as our Saviour. It directs us to see the truth of the Resurrection, as we see Jesus continuing his work through the members of the Church, his body. The Resurrection has made it possible for that life to be spread all over the world and all time.

The readings from Revelation during this Easter season continue to give us glimpses of resurrection life in the context of eternity, where there is lasting healing and total wholeness.

Fifth Sunday of Easter

Thought for the day

Christ, breaking through the barrier of sin and death, allows us to break into an entirely new way of living which continues into eternity.

Reflection on the readings

Acts 11:1-18; Psalm 148
Revelation 21:1-6; John 13:31-35

Today's readings continue to help us see events from several viewpoints at once. Rather like those remarkable holograms which burst into three dimensions from a flat surface, we are seeing the Crucifixion and Resurrection of Christ from beforehand, afterwards and in eternity, and these viewpoints, clustered together like this, throw into relief for us the powerful and cosmic significance of those events.

In the Gospel reading, just after Judas has gone out into the night, Jesus looks ahead to the imminent suffering, degradation and failure, and paradoxically claims that the Son of Man is about to be glorified. This is followed by the command given to his disciples to love one another. It is in their self-giving love that people will recognise their allegiance to the God who is glorified by this total expending of self about to be displayed on the cross. God will be glorified by the living-out of forgiving love without limit.

The reading from Revelation enables us to see from heaven's point of view, standing aside from the confines of time, and looking with the eyes of the visionary. There are images of accomplishment and victory over all evil for all time. There is the beginning of what is new, as if we are watching with the shepherds the self-emptying of God in the baby on manger straw, and the sense of that full completion at the end of time when all tears will be wiped away for ever. And stretched across time and space is the God of life, focused in the stretching-out of Jesus' arms for us on the cross.

Barriers crumble in the face of such love, and we see an example of this ongoing process in the reading from Acts, as Peter proclaims and celebrates his realisation that God's saving love is not confined to the Jewish people but is freely available to us all, however distant in years or miles we may be. As Christ breaks through the barrier of death, all new things become possible. If we are resurrection people, our lives will act this out and gather others into the kingdom through the way we refuse to live by the old order of sin, the old prejudices, the old values. Love, though expensive, is the new way to live, and we are to spread it liberally and lavishly without boundaries or exceptions.

Sixth Sunday of Easter

Thought for the day

The continuing presence of God, as Holy Spirit,
leads us, as Jesus promised,
into a personally guided outreach to all nations.

Reflection on the readings

Acts 16:9-15; Psalm 67
Revelation 21:10, 22-22:5; John 14:23-29 or John 5:1-9

During this time between the Resurrection and the Ascension Jesus continues to prepare his friends for something which is completely beyond their experience. In today's Gospel we hear how he introduces them to the idea of God's personal involvement through the power of the Holy Spirit. The prospect of having to carry on without Jesus in person among them must have been bleak and daunting to the disciples. Jesus speaks into those fears and assures them of this faithful presence once he has gone from their physical sight.

There is a section of the Bayeux tapestry which is called 'William encourages his soldiers'. This strikes me as a somewhat wry comment, as the picture shows William encouraging them by jabbing at their backsides with a sharp weapon! Forceful encouragement, indeed. But there is in this image an acknowledgement that fear can prevent us from doing what we know is right, and at such times a prod or two sharpens our determination to get the better of our fear.

When Jesus has given us full assurance of God's presence, we are told not to let our hearts be troubled. I suspect this has a sharper edge which is often missed, and we are actually being told not to allow ourselves to be perturbed or shaken by circumstances. Satan can so easily sidle in through our fear, self-doubt and trepidation, and start whispering the lie that whatever we are facing is far too difficult and we are bound to fail. We can prevent that, in God's strength, by refusing to allow such undermining fears access.

In the Acts reading we can see the promised guiding power of the Holy Spirit in action. God's close involvement with his people means that, whenever Christians are attuned to him and make themselves available, they will be led at the right time into the right circumstances where they can be best used for the work of God.

There is an urgency about outreach. We have before us that great vision of all peoples gathering to acknowledge their Creator, and worship the one true God, and whenever we pray the kingdom in, in the Lord's prayer, we voice our longing for the vision to be accomplished.

Yet there is still so much to do, so many lives to touch, and each of us has only a lifetime. Dare we waste any more of it with our own priorities?

Ascension Day

Thought for the day

Having bought back our freedom
with the giving of his life,
Jesus enters into the full glory
to which he is entitled.

Reflection on the readings

Acts 1:1-11 or Daniel 7:9-14
Psalm 47 or Psalm 93
Ephesians 1:15-23 or Acts 1:1-11
Luke 24:44-53

The Ascension marks the end of Jesus' appearances on earth and his physical, historical ministry. It is also a beginning, because this moving away from the confining qualities of time and place means that Jesus will be present always and everywhere. It also means that the humanity of Jesus is now within the nature of the wholeness of God. Our God has scarred hands and feet, and knows what it is like to be severely tempted, acclaimed and despised.

In a way, it is at the Ascension that the value of all the risk and suffering involved in the Incarnation becomes apparent. The saving victim takes his rightful place in the glory of heaven, and only that can enable God's Holy Spirit to be poured out in wave upon wave of loving power that stretches to all peoples in all generations.

Amazingly our own parish, our own congregation, is part of this glorious celebration with its far-reaching effects. Each of us, living squashed into a particular time frame lasting merely a lifetime, can be drenched in the power of that Spirit, and caught up in the energising nature of it.

As we celebrate the Ascension we, like the disciples, are expectant with joy at the prospect of the gifts God has in store, and yet still mulling over the breathtaking events of Easter. It is like being in the still centre, in the eye of the storm.

Seventh Sunday of Easter

Thought for the day

Jesus lives for all time in glory;
we can live the fullness of Resurrection
life straightaway.

Reflection on the readings

Acts 16:16-34; Psalm 97
Revelation 22:12-14, 16-17, 20-21; John 17:20-26

As we reach the final part of Jesus' great prayer before his arrest, recorded with perception and empathy by John, we cannot fail to be moved by the heartfelt yearning shown there. Jesus truly loves this untidy band of companions, and longs passionately for them to become bound to their God and to one another as they have already begun to in his company. And then we suddenly find that we, too, are being prayed for by our Saviour on the night before he dies. We are the ones who have come to believe through the witness of the apostles, and the years between melt away as we become aware of the personal handing-on in succession, one to another down through the generations from these friends to whoever it was who introduced us to Jesus.

There is a great air of excitement in the readings today, because we don't have to wait to start living this new Resurrection life Jesus promised. Pentecost is only a week away, the Lord reigns, Jesus in glory is also close with us, and the joy of living the risen life is infectious, as the marvellous reading from Acts shows.

In these days before celebrating Pentecost we see the effects of Pentecost, graphically described by Luke. It seems that Paul and Silas were at first content to let the slave girl direct people to the truth about them, but as it went on for days they must have found it getting to them. The imprisoning effect of this spirit on the poor girl must also have been increasingly obvious. Ironically, it is for liberating someone that the friends are beaten black and blue and thrown into prison.

And what do they do? They sit bruised and bleeding in the painful stocks and sing their hearts out, praising God! That is living the new life. That unquenchable, bubbling joy in real, lasting things is what other people notice and are attracted to. That night it changed the lives of the jailer and his entire family, and quite possibly some of the other prisoners as well.

Pentecost

Thought for the day

As Jesus promised, the Holy Spirit is poured out on the apostles and the Church is born.

Reflection on the readings

Acts 2:1-21 or Genesis 11:1-9; Psalm 104:24-34, 35b
Romans 8:14-17 or Acts 2:1-21; John 14:8-17 (25-27)

In the ancient story of Babel a deep human puzzle is explored. Why is it that, whenever we let our skills and gifts divert us into pride and ambition, we end up bickering and losing our capacity for mutual co-operation? It is a story which provides a useful foil to the events of Pentecost.

For here we have God's answer, and the Babel story turned on its head. God's Holy Spirit, residing in our whole being, opens up the possibility of living as God intended – in harmony with our Creator. That new relationship is bound to spill out into our relationships with one another, and work against the destructiveness we know so well and despair of overcoming.

As the force of the Spirit, coming in great power, surges like wind and fire into the place where the apostles are expectantly waiting, they are completely drenched in the waves of God's energising love. 'Drenched' is perhaps an odd word to use in the context of tongues of flame, but in terms of the Holy Spirit it makes sense, because air (breath or wind), water and fire – those raw experiences of natural power – are all linked with the physical expressions of the presence and power of God among his people.

It is God's nature to warn us ahead of time if something is coming up that he wants us seriously to attend to. The disciples have taken Jesus' prophecy to heart, and have been waiting watchfully and prayerfully for the last nine days since the Ascension. So often we miss God's voice because we are not expecting to hear it. We miss the outpouring of his Spirit in our lives because we are not expecting him to act. Yet as soon as we set ourselves faithfully and expectantly to ask for it and wait for it, God honours the honesty of our longing, and makes his presence known.

Trinity Sunday

Thought for the day

The unique nature of God is celebrated today,
as we reflect on the truth that God is Creator,
Redeemer and Life-giver.

Reflection on the readings

Proverbs 8:1-4, 22-31; Psalm 8
Romans 5:1-5; John 16:12-15

The actual word 'Trinity' does not occur in the Bible, but that is not to say it is not mentioned. As we get to understand the nature of God more and more, it becomes clear that we are wrestling with understanding something quite beyond our human experience. Even though God can make himself and his will known clearly to us along the way of life, there is no way that we will ever be able to grasp exactly who God is and what he is like, at least during our time on earth.

But that's no reason for not trying! Trying to get to grips with the truth about God's nature is all part of our journey into the depth of his being, and as such is immensely valuable. Our readings today are a good starting point.

First we have the poetry of Proverbs, expressing something of the 'community' of God's nature; the way that Wisdom, described as a personality, has been present from the very beginning, and was part of the creative loving process that brought all things into being. There is a sense of harmony and shared delight, along with the everlasting 'now', which we, being time-trapped, find hard to imagine.

Psalm 8 catches the song of Proverbs and dances with it, amazed at the nature of creation and the attitude of God towards it. Humankind is so privileged in having the ability to marvel.

In Romans we sense the orchestration of God; the way that in Jesus it all comes together, and we as humans can be drawn into God's life-giving power which transforms our attitudes to the trials and troubles we are likely to face. God is both transcendent and immanent.

So, when we read in John about Jesus referring to the Friend – the Spirit who will take his followers by the hand and lead them into the truth – in the same breath as he speaks about the Father and himself sharing all things, we can begin to glimpse something of the dynamics of God. Rather as you may look at a speck of microfilm and see it first as a dot which then explodes into a wealth of information when properly viewed, so our initial glimpses of God are going to burst into a dynamic, unimaginable richness which is sensed and worshipped, rather than understood.

Proper 4

Sunday between 29 May and 4 June inclusive
(if after Trinity Sunday)

Thought for the day

The good news we have been given is not just for us, but to pass on to the rest of the world.

Reflection on the readings

1 Kings 18:20-21 (22-29), 30-39 or 1 Kings 8:22-23, 41-43
Psalm 96 or Psalm 96:1-9
Galatians 1:1-12; Luke 7:1-10

When Jesus commissioned his apostles to go out and make disciples of all nations, he was not breaking with Jewish tradition but taking it one stage further. There had always been the understanding amongst God's chosen people that eventually through them the whole earth would be blessed, and all nations would come to realise that the God of Israel was the one and only God.

We see that in Psalm 96 today, in the fervent prayer of King Solomon, and in the story of Elijah and the prophets' competition when, as a result of what the people saw, they spontaneously turned to worship Elijah's powerful God who had shown himself to be listening and active. All these writings from the Old Testament assume that the truth is for everyone to share.

In the letter to the Church in Galatia it is clear that Paul has been putting into practice the command of Jesus to preach the good news to all nations. He had founded this church community during his first missionary journey, and encouraged the pagans to accept the sovereignty of the living God in their lives. Now he is finding that some of them are being persuaded that in order to become proper Christians they must also be brought under the Jewish Law. Passionately Paul writes to prevent the new freedom in Christ from being clawed back into the past confines of the legalistic traditions of Judaism.

In contrast, we find the army officer, who is not even Jewish, displaying a degree of faith that Jesus finds amazing.

Today's readings raise questions for us about who we should be evangelising, and what expectations we should have concerning rules and traditions, in view of where the unchurched are coming from. What shines out clearly is that outsiders are best persuaded of the truth about God by the behaviour of his followers and the amount of access they allow him into their lives.

Proper 5

Sunday between 5 and 11 June inclusive
(if after Trinity Sunday)

Thought for the day

Our God is full of compassion;
he hears our crying and it is his nature to rescue us.

Reflection on the readings

1 Kings 17:8-16 (17-24) or 1 Kings 17:17-24
Psalm 146 or Psalm 30
Galatians 1:11-24; Luke 7:11-17

Look at a picture of any person's face and you will see that one side speaks more of the hope and happiness and the other side more of the pain and suffering they have known. Although there is widespread expectation that we should be happy in life, the truth is that life is always a mixture of light and deep shadow, and our calling as humans is not so much to be happy as to be real.

God reaches down into our deep shadows and feels with us in the grieving and emptiness there. We see examples of that practical compassion in the readings from Kings and from Luke. With great tenderness, God provides not only for his friend and servant, Elijah, but also for the widow in Zarephath and her son. The flour and oil which never run out are like a sign of God's faithfulness to his people which also never fails.

As God's close friend, Elijah has that same love for people, which is poured out in prayer as he pleads for the child's life. Love is like a channel that cuts through any situation and allows God's healing to happen. Even those who have not received physical healing witness to the way that, through the prayers of faithful people, God has healed their anxiety or their attitude, and enabled them to face their suffering courageously. Many sense that they are being 'carried through' a difficult time.

When Jesus sees the heartbroken widow, with her dead son being carried out of the house, we are told he is filled with compassion, and it is out of this loving that he acts, speaking right into death and calling the young man back, for a while longer, into earthly life with his mother.

In a sense God calls all his people out of death. He calls us into the possibility of a life in which we are no longer living to the old rules of selfishness, but are freed to walk tall in the light and life of God's loving.

Proper 6

Sunday between 12 and 18 June inclusive
(if after Trinity Sunday)

Thought for the day

God has the authority and the desire
to forgive our sins completely
and set us free from guilt.

Reflection on the readings

1 Kings 21:1-10 (11-14), 15-21a
or 2 Samuel 11:26-12:10, 13-15; Psalm 5:1-8 or Psalm 32
Galatians 2:15-21; Luke 7:36-8:3

Most of the time it is not so much a falling into sin as a sliding into sin that happens. Ahab did not simply wake up one morning and decide to have Jezebel sort Naboth out, and David was not the kind of person to stick one of his men deliberately in the front line to have him out of the way. We slip gradually towards committing the terrible wrongs by not paying attention to the top of the slide – sins of pride, greed, laziness and self-indulgence, for instance – which if unchecked will start us sliding further and further into wrong values and wrong behaviour.

Since the slide is often so gradual, we may not notice what is happening, and our readings today show us some examples of the ways God does his best to draw our attention to what needs putting right. Being in the position of God's spokesperson at such times is an unenviable job, but a very necessary one. We may well prefer to wriggle out of the responsibility with the excuse that we don't want to be judgemental. But to avoid alerting someone to a downward slide in their lives is actually unloving behaviour. If we ensure that we do it in love, and without being judgemental, it is one of the kindest acts we can do.

Once our attention is drawn to the wrong we have done, or the wrong attitudes we have allowed to become habits, we are faced with a choice. Since it is never pleasant to be faced with criticism, and we have probably put considerable energy into persuading ourselves that our behaviour and attitudes are justifiable, we may wish to go on the defensive, and reject what we have been shown. If we choose that route God is unable to put things right for us.

If, on the other hand, we are honest enough to see some truth in what has been said, we can take that great and difficult step of breaking down our defences before God and acknowledging that we need him to sort things out. God is the only one with the authority to forgive sin completely, and he is very good at it. The other thing about him is that he loves doing it, and will help us as much as possible.

The only way of crawling back to the top of the slide is recognising and acknowledging before God what is wrong, taking full responsibility for it, and expressing our shame and sorrow – our desire to stop and change. It is those who have known the incredible release and joy of God's forgiveness in large measure who have great love for the one who has let them out of their prison.

Proper 7

Sunday between 19 and 25 June inclusive
(if after Trinity Sunday)

Thought for the day

God is close through all our troubles,
and can bring us safely through them.

Reflection on the readings

1 Kings 19:1-4 (5-7), 8-15a or Isaiah 65:1-9
Psalms 42, 43 or Psalm 22:19-28
Galatians 3:23-29; Luke 8:26-39

In the readings today there is no shortage of heartaches. And for many people, it comes as a relief to find that Christianity addresses the pains, troubles and heartaches of life, not by telling us these things shouldn't matter; not by giving us good advice on how to get out of any pit we are in; but by providing a person who is prepared to climb down into the pit with us. For that is what we need at such times, and all we can cope with.

Let's look at Elijah who had so courageously challenged the prophets of Baal, and is now drained and vulnerable, probably exhausted, and temporarily crushed by the powerful dominance of the scheming Queen Jezebel. It looks to him as if everything he has lived and worked for has fallen about his ears, and that, as many of us know from experience, is a desolate place to be.

I love the way God deals with Elijah. First the practical, sensible caring: Elijah is taken to a safe place and given sleep, food, more sleep and more food! Thank heavens for all those practical caring Christians who act out this kind of loving without any questions or deliberations or advice at this stage! Then he is given space and time to come to God at his own pace. We are in such danger of trying to rush healing, with all the counselling piled on at times of heartache, forgetting this need which our God always remembers. Any grief takes time, and we must be prepared to give others that time.

Then comes the close contact, when Elijah is ready for it. Gently God brings him to state the ache, and that may need to be stated more than once. God only continues when he can see Elijah has no further need to state it. Now Elijah is ready to move forward, so it is only now that God gives direction, encouragement and assurance.

What heartache there must have been in the country of the Gerasene people over this wild man, and what turmoil and terror in the man himself. Jesus, with the honesty of love, makes contact with the agonised being trapped inside the horror. The healing holds its own horror, as the drowning pigs give us some idea of the power that had been strangling the sanity of the man. And the people cannot cope. Yet Jesus again gives a commissioning to the released man, knowing that the people need their time and space to come gradually to understand and receive his teaching.

There is much here that we can learn about our own encounters with those whose hearts are heavy.

Proper 8

Sunday between 26 June and 2 July inclusive

Thought for the day

When we are called to follow Jesus, that means total commitment, with no half-measures.

Reflection on the readings

2 Kings 2:1-2, 6-14 or 1 Kings 19:15-16, 19-21
Psalm 77:1-2, 11-20 or Psalm 16
Galatians 5:1, 13-25; Luke 9:51-62

Both the readings from Kings describe Elisha's calling, first to be Elijah's servant and disciple, and then his successor. In each case the cloak is an important sign of authority and acceptance, and Elisha chooses to take up the mantle, with all the commitment that this involves.

In the reading from Luke other people are called to follow Jesus, and not everyone is prepared to do this. Others enthusiastically offer to come with him, and Jesus has to dampen their enthusiasm somewhat by bringing them down to earth, and making them count the cost of the commitment before they decide. The practical living arrangements, for instance, and probable lack of home comforts, need to be looked squarely in the face before the choice is made.

It is not everyone's calling to wander with Jesus around the countryside, preaching and healing the sick. Equally valid is the ministry of those chatting the good news among their own people in their own towns and villages, and of all those living by God's values in commerce and industry. What binds all these people together, though, is the decision made to commitment.

In the baptismal promises the Church continues to place people on the spot. What commitment to Christ entails is stated clearly, so there may be no misunderstanding, and the candidates are free to choose whether to commit themselves or not. But, having made the choice, there is no getting away from the fact that they are committed to living differently.

As Paul explains to the Galatians, it is for *our* freedom that Christ has set us free, and to settle back into former sin patterns will only enslave us. Living as committed Christians we need to check constantly that we are still walking in step with the Spirit. Paul gives us a whole list of examples to check our behaviour against, so that we can adjust our direction accordingly.

Proper 9

Sunday between 3 and 9 July inclusive

Thought for the day

In Christ we become a new creation.

Reflection on the readings

2 Kings 5:1-14 or Isaiah 66:10-14; Psalm 30 or Psalm 66:1-9
Galatians 6:(1-6) 7-16; Luke 10:1-11, 16-20

At first Naaman is most reluctant to take the necessary steps for his skin to be made new. Elisha's instructions are far too low-tech and simple for a man of his standing and intelligence. It's all rather an insult. Yet he was anxious enough to be healed. The skin disease was both irritating and unsightly, and judging by the changes of clothing packed for the journey, Naaman was a fastidious man.

Happily his servants are able to persuade him to put his pride away and try the recommended cure, and he is totally thrilled with the result. We sense his joy and relief as he comes up out of the water with skin as clear as a young child's.

God can give us all that 'fresh as a young child' sensation, as we allow him to make us new creations, born of the Spirit. Paul, writing to the Galatians, sees that a constant battle is going on between our sinful nature and our spiritual nature, and inspires us to go for the better deal of the spiritual nature, which brings joy and lasts for eternity. It is bringing people to enjoy this new creation which is the whole point of our ministry, says Paul, and the religious traditions and habits matter only in so far as they help to make us aware of our need of God's nursing and bathing. The really important thing is being made new.

And there are so many tired and disillusioned souls, all struggling to save themselves, and suspecting their frenetic attempts are actually doomed to failure, if they dared stop for a minute and look. Jesus sees it as a huge harvest, ripe for gathering, but with far too few workers; and people remain trapped in their distracted existence as a result of meeting no one able to offer them the freedom of God's new life.

So today offers us both great hope and a great challenge. Who are the workers to be?

Proper 10

Sunday between 10 and 16 July inclusive

Thought for the day

Straighten your lives out and live by God's standards of love.

Reflection on the readings

Amos 7:7-17 or Deuteronomy 30:9-14
Psalm 82 or Psalm 25:1-10
Colossians 1:1-14; Luke 10:25-37

It is in today's Psalms that God's standards of loving are clearly and beautifully stated. These precepts of defending the cause of the poor and oppressed, upholding right judgement and caring for those in need, are like a strong heartbeat pulsing underneath the events and stories of the other readings.

Amos, burning with God's indignation at the corruption and idolatry of the practices in the northern kingdom, sees the lives they have built like a leaning wall that ought to be straight and true. Not surprisingly his words, spoken as an outsider from the southern kingdom, and critical of a civilisation which has brought comfort and wealth to many, are received with anger and verbal abuse. It's never an easy life being a prophet. Amos bridles in response. Surely they didn't think he would have chosen to come to their country? Their refusal to listen to God's warning simply proves the extent of their spiritual deafness, which is bound to bring about their destruction.

In the reading from Luke, Jesus is also facing opposition. The seventy-two have recently arrived back, and there has no doubt been an angry backlash from those towns denounced by Jesus for their refusal to receive the message brought to them. The law expert is smugly deprecating as he leads Jesus into a trap, which Jesus neatly sidesteps, dropping the man in instead. Perhaps he was hoping for Jesus to agree that 'neighbour' only refers to those within the law – such as the denounced Capernaum, for instance?

The story Jesus gives by way of an answer forces him to look with God's measure, or plumb line, at attitudes and assumptions which need a thorough overhaul. The right words may still be in place, so that love for God and neighbour can be glibly quoted, but the spirit of those words has dried up inside and left only the empty shell.

In contrast, Paul is full of thankfulness at the lush growth of the Christians at Colossae, and he prays for that to continue to flourish. For us, too, there are many signs of regrowth and regeneration in the Church, which is wonderful to see. We need to ensure that walls are regularly checked as we build, so they can stay true to God's priorities and values.

And when any prophet speaks out, and what they say is uncomfortable to hear, it is wise to listen carefully, in case the unpalatable is the truth. Prophecy is rather like a surgeon's scalpel: it's worth putting up with being sliced open if it leads to healing and life, rather than death by default.

Proper 11

Sunday between 17 and 23 July inclusive

Thought for the day

Against impossible odds God has reconciled us to himself, in Christ.

Reflection on the readings

Amos 8:1-12 or Genesis 18:1-10a
Psalm 52 or Psalm 15
Colossians 1:15-28; Luke 10:38-42

This week we are given a near-lethal dose of the bad news about human nature. The prophecy from Amos is particularly bleak and depressing because it paints such a true picture of the familiar materialistic, self-orientated world we know, both in society and in the secret places of our own hearts.

What hope can there possibly be? As humans we hold on to a vision of what it ought to be, and how we ought to live, but the disturbing truth is that we seem unable to haul ourselves above the selfish nature that drives us. We may see glimpses of nobility here and there in good men and women doing better than the rest of us, but the main tide is in the other direction, with no real possibility of widespread goodness. In Amos we read of that terrible prophecy of a famine, worse than thirst and hunger, which speaks of us being abandoned for our failure and locked out from all hope, as people struggle and search for the word of the Lord but never find it.

Into this misery and helplessness strides Paul, through his letter to the Colossians, like a being from a new and different dimension, shouting to us over the centuries that we need not despair. Someone has done the impossible, and through Christ Jesus, stretched out between earth and heaven in love, God has been able to reconcile all things to himself. Far from being abandoned, he has been searching through the rubble and debris of our human situation and has come in person to rescue us.

Proper 12

Sunday between 24 and 30 July inclusive

Thought for the day

Keep asking for God's Spirit
and he will keep pouring out
his blessing on you.

Reflection on the readings

Hosea 1:2-10 or Genesis 18:20-32; Psalm 85 or Psalm 138
Colossians 2:6-15 (16-19); Luke 11:1-13

It is not God's will that anyone should be lost; God longs for all of us to be saved. Each one of the inhabitants of Sodom and Gomorrah was part of God's loving creation, and made in his image. Each person in Israel was known and loved. Those in every generation, who deliberately turn away and feed their selfish nature until they can no longer hear God's prompting, are all cherished and of God's making.

Today's readings remind us of that immense parental tenderness that God has for us. He creates us full of potential and watches over our spiritual growth, ready to bathe us in his light, and drench us in his Spirit. The tragedy is that we so often refuse to let him give us the gifts necessary for our growth.

In the Genesis reading we are given this lovely example of the close relationship shared by Abraham with his God. He is full of respect, and perfectly understands the justice of the threatened destruction, but he feels with his God's love the terrible sadness of waste, and pleads for mercy on behalf of those cities. How his pleading must have made God's heart sing, for here was a man loving in the broad and generous way he longed to see in all his creation.

The passage from Paul's letter to the Colossians urges his readers to let their growth in faith continue to flourish in Christ so that their lives overflow with thankfulness. It is not a question of everything happening at the beginning of our journey when we first commit ourselves. To grow, and to remain in close fellowship with God, we need constant filling up, feeding and guiding on a daily basis. The Bible, prayer and communion are gifts provided for us to use, and without taking God up on these gifts, our spiritual growth will weaken and become stunted.

In the Gospel for today, the disciples ask Jesus to teach them to pray, and the guidelines they are given have been valued by Christians of all denominations and traditions through the centuries. Luke links this teaching on prayer with a whole passage encouraging us to ask for what we need, and ask persistently. God will never force himself on anyone; he waits for us to invite him into our lives, and that is why it is so vital that we do ask and seek and knock at the door.

If we look at many of his acts of healing, we find Jesus often gets people to state what they want; that is part of the healing because God likes to work in partnership with us, not as a take-over bid. So he wants us to wake up each morning and ask that the kingdom may come, that we may have our daily needs provided – both physical and spiritual – and that we may have our sins forgiven and be guided safely through temptation. That way we shall be actively seeking the God who made us and loves us, and has ready all the gifts we need to bear fruit.

Proper 13

Sunday between 31 July and 6 August inclusive

Thought for the day

True richness is not material wealth;
true security is not a financial matter.

Reflection on the readings

Hosea 11:1-11 or Ecclesiastes 1:2, 12-14; 2:18-23
Psalm 107:1-9, 43 or Psalm 49:1-12
Colossians 3:1-11; Luke 12:13-21

Our culture runs on consumerism, and one of the side-effects of that is an encouragement of greed and increase in the daily temptation through the media to us that security, happiness and peace of mind come from possessions and self-indulgence. It is a myth which has enough truth in it to be dangerous. It undoubtedly helps to have enough to live on, but the wisdom of Mr Micawber holds true, all the same: living within our means is happiness where finances are concerned, and sixpence over that is misery! Many know the misery of accumulated debts resulting from the pressure to live beyond our means and spend what we actually haven't got.

It is a short step from being told that we haven't got something to believing we need (rather than want) it, especially if we can see others who already have it. The 'if only's set in, with their accompanying sense of discontent and resentment. Equally dangerous is the possession of financial 'security' which can kid us that we have no need of God, so that we shut down our spiritual antennae and grow increasingly oblivious to the needs of others and the glaring inequalities. The preoccupation with protecting what we own is good news for the insurance and home security firms, but bad news for the soul.

Today's readings point out the foolishness of living in this way, and the wisdom of living with our security in the eternal things. Now that Christ has given us a new life, our insurance – or perhaps I should say 'assurance' – is kept with Christ in heaven. The whole yardstick of life is changed, and our time here recognised as only the first part of our full and lasting life. When we really grasp the implications of what Jesus has done for us, it is bound to alter our outlook on what is important to possess and what is of only minimal value.

It is not so much a question of giving away our possessions as changing our attitude to them and recognising them for what they are – pleasant comforts to thank God for, but lent to us to use, as good stewards, and in no way altering our real wealth and security.

Proper 14

Sunday between 7 and 13 August inclusive

Thought for the day

Have faith in God,
and get yourself ready to meet him.

Reflection on the readings

Isaiah 1:1, 10-20; Psalm 50:1-8, 22-23
Hebrews 11:1-3, 8-16; Luke 12:32-40

The Gospel reading for today begins with such an affectionate reassurance. It is God's good pleasure and delight to give us the kingdom; everything is in hand, and nothing can ever tear us apart from the God who loves us. The only way separation can happen is by us choosing to walk away ourselves. So our God has us safe and expectant, knowing that there are great things in store for us both in this world and the next, even though we cannot see them.

That is the faith God looks for in his people: believing the hope as a fact and trusting that what God has promised will indeed happen. The reading from Hebrews recalls the extraordinary faith of Abraham, God's close friend, in the way he was prepared to launch out into the unknown on many occasions, simply because God told him to. Not only did he believe that God had authority which asked for obedience; he also knew that God's responsible, caring nature would ensure that placing himself in the hands of his Lord was a sensible and safe thing to do.

So Abraham's faith determined how he lived. That always happens; you cannot trust the one true God and go on behaving with corruption, deceit, injustice or self-glory which you know to be totally alien to his nature. But it is, of course, perfectly possible to pretend you have faith, and go through the rituals of words and worship, while your eyes stoically avoid God's gaze, and your life proclaims that you actually despise the one you claim to worship.

It was exactly this which so wounded the heart of God about the people of Israel, to whom Isaiah was sent. How could God accept their offerings when they were living a lie? Hypocrisy and corruption creep up on us insidiously, minor detail by minor detail, so that we end up fooling ourselves that wrong is right. Sometimes we can fool others, too. But God we do not fool, and his reaction is to try to shake us out of the lie we are in, because he hates us being there and knows it causes all kinds of stress, whether we recognise that or not.

Having faith means looking seriously at the God we claim to believe in, and checking that our lives, in every aspect, in secret and in the open, are lined up with those qualities of truth, love, integrity and right action which are hallmarks of God and his friends.

Proper 15

Sunday between 14 and 20 August inclusive

Thought for the day

When we fix our eyes on Jesus
our lives will reflect his nature.

Reflection on the readings

Isaiah 5:1-7 or Jeremiah 23:23-29
Psalm 80:1-2, 8-19 or Psalm 82
Hebrews 11:29-12:2; Luke 12:49-56

Many parents have high hopes for their children. Musical toys are given encouragingly to offspring who start singing in tune before they can talk. Balls to kick around are bought partly for fun and partly to foster any latent talent. Financial sacrifices are made for children showing potential in particular sports or arts. It would be cynical to think that all this is 'pushy parent syndrome'; mostly it shows the natural pride and delight of parents in the children they love.

God, too, has high hopes for the children he loves. He delights in our progress, and looks out for the seeds of gifts he has given us to blossom; he loves to watch us using these gifts for the good of the world. Today we sense God's sadness as he looks for the good and wholesome we are capable of as his creation, and finds instead destructive selfishness, bloodshed and cries of distress. We all know the aching disappointment of an attempt which has failed, in spite of the lavish care we have invested in it. Sadly we have to recognise that sometimes our behaviour, both collectively and individually, disappoints our parent God.

Such behaviour and attitudes are a waste of our life. The writer of the letter to the Hebrews urges us to get rid of everything that hinders and entangles us, so that we can run the race more easily and comfortably. And the best way of doing that is by keeping our sights fixed on Jesus. It is noticeable throughout history that whenever people have done this they have been enabled to bring about great good, both within the Church and in society. It is when their eyes swivel round to fix on other things that corruption, distortion of truth, and injustice start taking over. Like bindweed, they can look attractive, but throttle the life out of whatever they climb over. And the roots need to be totally eradicated to prevent strong regrowth. Jesus warns his followers that the path of righting deep-rooted wrong will not be straightforward or without radical disturbance and upheaval, not only in individuals, but also in families and nations and church communities.

Proper 16

Sunday between 21 and 27 August inclusive

Thought for the day

God sets his leaders apart to challenge prejudices and assumptions, and alert people to the truth.

Reflection on the readings

Jeremiah 1:4-10 or Isaiah 58:9b-14
Psalm 71:1-6 or Psalm 103:1-8
Hebrews 12:18-29; Luke 13:10-17

The crippled woman, who made her way into the synagogue on that Sabbath day, would have had her eyes, as always, fixed on the floor in front of her. Her bent back meant that she had to put up with a very narrow field of vision. When Jesus released her spine to move from its locked position, she could at last look ahead, up and around with a wonderful new freedom, which thrilled her and set her praising God. Her life would have changed completely now that her 'outlook' had been so freed.

Others in that congregation were equally locked, with a cripplingly narrow field of spiritual vision. They had reduced the keeping of the Law to a complicated set of detailed rules, and had spent so much energy focusing on these that they could no longer see the spirit and essence of the Law, guiding people to love God and love one another. When they were faced with the possibility of being released from their narrow field of vision, they could see it only in terms of broken rules.

Not only Jesus, but also all the prophets of the Old Testament and all those commissioned from the New Testament down to today, are called by God to speak out and challenge people's assumptions and prejudices – to straighten the spiritual backs of the narrowly visioned. God longs for his people to be free, and wherever people have become spiritually jammed, God raises up someone to offer them release and a fresh start.

Today we are urged to take God up on his offer of release and new vision, and not to miss out on the possibility of our whole life and outlook being transformed just because we have become used to behaving in a particular way. As the crippled woman found, it's worth straightening up.

Proper 17

Sunday between 28 August and 3 September inclusive

Thought for the day

When we live God's way, both individually and as a community, we will be greatly blessed.

Reflection on the readings

Jeremiah 2:4-13 or Ecclesiasticus 10:12-18
Psalm 81:1, 10-16 or Psalm 112
Hebrews 13:1-8, 15-16; Luke 14:1, 7-14

In the reading from Jeremiah there is a powerful image of a broken, leaking well. God grieves because his people have chosen to reject the life-giving springs of his pure water which never dry up, and decided instead to do their own thing and build these wells which are cracked, so any water they collect quickly runs away. The wells of their own making are vastly inferior and they don't work; yet still the people choose to trust these, rather than God's blatantly superior offer.

Often when people are first converted, they are bursting to tell people about the God they have just discovered, and can't understand how anyone could not want what they have found, even though for years they themselves have also been struggling with leaking wells without realising the reality of God's alternative. The more Christians there are gossiping the good news among their own contacts in a regular, informal and friendly way, the more chance there is of people hearing about God's offer at the point when their hearts are ready to listen.

It was at a 'Sunday dinner' equivalent, as one of the guests, that Jesus brought the conversation round to what people needed to hear, spoken anecdotally and through the after-dinner stories. They described a way of thinking that was quite radical, turning accepted values upside-down and suggesting a way of living which could liberate people and transform them.

The reading from Hebrews provides us with some good, practical guidelines for living God's way, both as individuals and as a community. All the behaviour described is a natural result of loving one another as brothers and sisters – as 'family'. We are advised to pray imaginatively for prisoners and all those who suffer – 'as if you are there with them'. There is a great sense of the importance of community, with the mutual care and respect that results from being bound together in love. Perhaps we need to recover some enthusiasm for community again, and recognise that in God's way of living, individuals have a calling and a responsibility to be members of a corporate unit of loving: the Church of God.

Proper 18

Sunday between 4 and 10 September inclusive

Thought for the day

Following Jesus is expensive –
it costs everything, but it's worth it.

Reflection on the readings

Jeremiah 18:1-11 or Deuteronomy 30:15-20
Psalm 139:1-6, 13-18 or Psalm 1
Philemon 1-21; Luke 14:25-33

No sooner have you missed paying a credit card bill than invitations to get further into borrowing start crashing through your letter box. We live in an age of plastic or electronic money where the planning of our finances is pressurised to include living beyond our means, and many discover, too late, that they have over-reached themselves and are heavily, and dangerously, in debt. Jesus' words from today's Gospel hit home to us very powerfully. It is so easy to start enthusiastically committing yourself financially to a new bathroom, car or double-glazing, and regret your decision once the 'pay later' date has arrived in the present.

Although Jesus' words sound very strict and demanding, they badly need to be taken on board. It is essential that no one is given the impression that following Jesus is all easy and happy, with no real cost involved. Part of spreading the good news is ensuring that people are properly informed of the small print. In fact Jesus would not have it in small print, but large letters, so there is no doubt about what is required in the way of commitment. God wants us to make a well-informed, well-considered decision; becoming a Christian, like undertaking marriage, should never be done lightly or carelessly.

Placing God at the centre of our lives means deliberately placing him at the centre of our thinking and working, our emotions and feelings, our energy and ambitions and in the centre of every relationship, and every decision. Just as when you look at the world through a coloured filter, everything is coloured, so when we take the decision to follow Jesus, everything is coloured by that commitment.

So far, so demanding! Of course, the wonderful good news is that when we take this step we can trust God to lead us into the very best, most fulfilling life possible. The lovely Psalm 139 celebrates the intimate knowledge God has of us, and every stage of our growing. Never will he demand of us less than we can, in his strength, give. Never will he push us too fast or overload us too quickly. In partnership with Jesus we can look forward to a lifetime of growing, blossoming and fruiting, in an environment of total security, warm affection and the knowledge of being precious and valuable.

Proper 19

Sunday between 11 and 17 September inclusive

Thought for the day

Jesus does not avoid the company of sinners but befriends them.

Reflection on the readings

Jeremiah 4:11-12, 22-28 or Exodus 32:7-14
Psalm 14 or Psalm 51:1-10
1 Timothy 1:12-17; Luke 15:1-10

Today's readings take us on a journey from near despair to strong hope. We begin with the Jeremiah passage, where we look the human condition full in the face and recognise the human capacity for making wrong, self-centred choices, excelling at mastering the skills of evil, and sidling away from the responsibility of godly living, preferring to indulge in the pursuit of personal comfort and the easy life. Ancient Judah could equally be the world in the twenty-first century.

How does a totally good and loving God cope? In Jesus we find out: God comes to the rescue, in person, searching out the lost, untangling them from the messy situations they have got themselves into, and carrying them safely home. The whole of heaven rejoices over each and every one.

In his letter to Timothy, Paul cites himself as living proof that God is indeed merciful and ready to forgive sinners, wherever they are coming from. He, after all, was actively persecuting the followers of Jesus when God alerted him to the truth and transformed his life. Many of us know the same truth in our own lives – I used to be a passionate atheist and now here I am writing this book! The Lord is an excellent shepherd and can find any bedraggled sheep, no matter where they have wandered off to, or how muddy and unsavoury they have become.

God will always search for us because he loves us, and doesn't want any of us to be lost. But it is still up to us whether or not we agree to be rescued.

Proper 20

Sunday between 18 and 24 September inclusive

Thought for the day

If you cannot be trusted with worldly riches,
or even small amounts of money,
then you will not be trusted
with spiritual riches either.

Reflection on the readings

Jeremiah 8:18-9:1 or Amos 8:4-7; Psalm 79:1-9 or Psalm 113
1 Timothy 2:1-7; Luke 16:1-13

Today's readings remind us that the way we deal with worldly finances and possessions should be scrupulously honest, fair and wise. It should be directly affected by our spiritual values, and reflect our beliefs completely.

The story of the cheating manager and his cunning way of avoiding trouble has the rich man praising him for his cleverness. This does not mean that Jesus is advising us all to follow the manager's example, of course, but it certainly highlights the zeal given to worldly affairs compared with the laid-back attitude so often given to eternal and spiritual matters. If we were to take the same trouble over our spiritual journey as criminals invest in embezzlement, the results would be dynamic in the extreme.

Jesus also picks up on our need to be responsible with our worldly affairs. It is no good excusing ourselves from such responsibilities on the grounds that we are only interested in spiritual things. Jesus is always practical, and realises that the way we manage our weekly budget, our expenses and our life-decisions is important. If we can't manage these honestly and sensibly, we are likely to be irresponsible about the important things of life as well.

Jeremiah was deeply saddened by his own people using their privileged position as a cover for ungodly behaviour. The closer we get to God's way of thinking, the more saddened we will be by the lack of integrity around us. We are bound to start noticing people's misdirected 'worth-ship' and longing for a change of direction. This sadness and yearning is all part of walking in step with the God who loves us and desires that sinners should turn and live.

Proper 21

Sunday between 25 September and 1 October inclusive

Thought for the day

Wealth can make us complacent so that we fail to notice the needs of those around us.

Reflection on the readings

Jeremiah 32:1-3a, 6-15 or Amos 6:1a, 4-7
Psalm 91:1-6, 14-16 or Psalm 146
1 Timothy 6:6-19; Luke 16:19-31

On the face of it, Jeremiah's purchase of the field was likely to be a complete waste of money. Had he been thinking only in terms of financial gain, it would hardly have been considered a wise investment. But since God had just spoken to him about using it as a sign of hope, Jeremiah was happy to go along with God's priorities. These took precedence over all his plans and ambitions.

Amos underlines for us the danger of being comfortably well off; the very comfort can cushion us from feeling for the poor and needy until we barely notice their suffering. So often this goes along with a sense of well-being which lulls us into thinking life is like this for everyone else too. We can become so cut off from the real world that we actually believe the needs are not there. It is this blindness, and the injustice of the situation, which angers the God of love and compassion. He feels for the ones who get despised and ignored, simply because they possess less.

Paul has more good advice for young Timothy. He, too, recognises that many sins can get traced back to the 'love of money' rootstock, and advises Timothy to stay well away from it, pursuing instead the kind of riches that are good and eternal. God is by far the better bargain!

The parable of the rich man and Lazarus focuses our minds on the seriousness and urgency of this whole question. We are not to know when our opportunities for living thoughtfully and generously will run out; it would be sensible to sort it all out now, while we still have the chance. As we take stock of how we are living, we can hold in front of us the picture of this wealthy man who did nothing particularly evil, but neglected to notice the needs of those he probably saw every day.

Proper 22

Sunday between 2 and 8 October inclusive

Thought for the day

God hears our distress and our crying,
and feels it with us.

Reflection on the readings

Lamentations 1:1-6 or Habakkuk 1:1-4; 2:1-4
Lamentations 3:19-26 or Psalm 137, or Psalm 37:1-9
2 Timothy 1:1-14; Luke 17:5-10

Today's readings are full of laments and heartbroken crying. Our faith is not a fair-weather faith, but speaks into our pain as well as our joy, into our darkest valleys as well as our hill-top experiences. It is both crucifixion and resurrection. God never does nothing when we pray; he may not come charging into the situation and sort it in the way we would like, but in his time, which is the best time, he will redeem it for good, and while we are waiting he will provide all the courage, inner peace and hope we need.

The important thing for us to establish as we cry is God's position in the suffering. So often when there are national tragedies we hear people crying, 'How could a loving God let this happen?' as if God were there orchestrating the evil or, even worse, watching it with his arms folded. This is a terrible distortion of the truth, for the real God of compassion is neither tyrannical, nor aloof and unconcerned. Nor is he well-intentioned but ineffectual. He is there suffering alongside the broken-hearted, sharing their grief and distress and ready to comfort them by being there. The costly gift of free will is matched by the costly gift of loving redemption.

At the same time, as today's Gospel reminds us, there is

no room for spiritual self-pity. We have no built-in rights for everything in our lives to run smoothly and easily, and Jesus is forthright in talking of the servant who simply accepts the work and weariness as part of his duty, without expecting any special payment or privileges. If following Christ brings us hardship and suffering, that is no more than we were told to expect, and we are asked to accept it as such, always on the understanding and conviction that we will be provided with whatever grace and strength we need to cope and triumph over the difficulties.

Proper 23

Sunday between 9 and 15 October inclusive

Thought for the day

God can always use even seemingly hopeless situations for good.

Reflection on the readings

Jeremiah 29:1, 4-7 or 2 Kings 5:1-3, 7-15
Psalm 66:1-12 or Psalm 111
2 Timothy 2:8-15; Luke 17:11-19

The people of Jerusalem have been taken into exile and forced to live far from home in the city of Babylon. They are aware of the unpleasant truth that this is at least partly their own fault, and in his letter to them, speaking out the word of God, Jeremiah urges them to think and act positively, so that through their presence in Babylon the city may be blessed. We have probably all known at some time the misery of being rejected and isolated. Whether we are in that place through our own fault or through circumstances beyond our control, it is still a bleak and painful place to be.

Some of us will have known the haunting suspicion that we could infect others, either physically or emotionally; most of us can only guess at the terrible sense of chronic isolation and terror experienced by those with leprosy.

Jesus meets the ten lepers in their community of isolation, outside one of the villages, and all their years of suffering pour out poignantly as they plead for pity from their contamination zone. Jesus, ever practical, tells them not that they are healed, but that they are to go and do what healed lepers have to do by law – show themselves to the priest. It is typical of godly direction to use the existing framework so as to bless as many people as possible.

Paul, writing to Timothy, is actually chained up in prison, but quite content to be there as anywhere else, because he knows that although he is chained, the good news is not, and can bring anyone blessing, wherever you happen to spread it.

This is rather heartening, because it means that all of us can blossom with God's love where we are planted; we don't have to wait until we are in a 'better' situation, or get discouraged because we only meet those in the office or on the bus each day. The wholesome goodness of the Gospel can be brought to those we meet – by us!

Proper 24

Sunday between 16 and 22 October inclusive

Thought for the day

Don't get side-tracked;
always pray and don't give up.

Reflection on the readings

Jeremiah 31:27-34 or Genesis 32:22-31
Psalm 119:97-104 or Psalm 121
2 Timothy 3:14-4:5; Luke 18:1-8

I have a half-finished tapestry somewhere in the back of a cupboard, which has been in that state for years. Whenever I rediscover it, I make the decision to keep it, as one day I may have the time to finish it. Even as I put it back in the cupboard I know this is unlikely; the commitment simply isn't there, as my tapestry doesn't rank high enough in my order of priorities.

For many people, faith in God is similarly packed away, and brought out and looked at from time to time. Their prayer-life is haphazard and irregular, with long gaps of inattentiveness punctuated with occasional attempts to open up the communication channels. For whatever reasons, building a deep relationship with God is simply not a high priority at present. If it were, the commitment would show in a regular and more persistent prayer pattern.

Whereas my tapestry remains much the same sitting in the cupboard, relationships are dynamic and do not store well without attention. It is always rather sad when a close friendship subsides into the printed Christmas letter category. Although this can be a valiant effort to avoid losing touch completely, it is a poor substitute for the daily contact and shared lives. And so often our prayer-life and Bible-reading, if similarly rare and impersonal, result in a very stilted relationship with God, which is a poor substitute for the rich, vibrant companionship he has in mind for us.

We live in a rather fragmented and disjointed culture, which doesn't help. Many young children are now entering school with a marked increase in poor listening and concentration skills. Persistence in anything, whatever it is, does not come easily. But prayer, like our heartbeat, needs to be regular and constant, a quiet rhythm pulsing faithfully under all our other activities. We also have a responsibility to keep up our study of the Bible so that we, like Timothy, are thoroughly equipped for every work.

Proper 25

Sunday between 23 and 29 October inclusive

Thought for the day

When we recognise our dependence on God
we will approach him with true humility
and accept his gifts with joy.

Reflection on the readings

Joel 2:23-32 or Ecclesiasticus 35:12-17 or
Jeremiah 14:7-10, 19-22; Psalm 65 or Psalm 84:1-7
2 Timothy 4:6-8, 16-18; Luke 18:9-14

We all want to be independent, and any parent can remember the battles which mark the route! One of the hardest things for the ageing is having to gradually relinquish their independence, and many struggle on with great difficulty rather than asking for help. This kind of pride in our independence as humans is good and healthy. The danger comes when we lose touch with where we have come from, and forget that as created beings we are fundamentally dependent on our creator and sustainer, God himself.

The readings today express the praise and thanksgiving which result from recognising God's lavish showering of gifts on his people. There is so much to be thankful for, and the whole pattern of seasonal rain and growth work as a visible sign of God's Spirit drenching and soaking us as it is poured out over us in life-giving abundance. Even those of us who have long been city-dwellers can appreciate the image of rain and growth.

To receive such a drenching we need to be like the earth, open and vulnerable, and ready to accept a soaking. It isn't any coincidence that the word 'humility' means 'earthiness'. And we simply can't be earthy if we are working on the principle that we have no need of God, or of anyone's help, and can manage perfectly well on our own, thank you.

While the Pharisee in today's Gospel is going through the motions of communicating with God, he is really affirming his own independent worth and has no concept of his deep need of God at all. It's like insisting on protecting our earth from rain; and if we do that, nothing can grow. In contrast the tax collector, complete with questionable morals and principles, at least recognises his basic dependence on God, and his need of God's mercy. It is this honesty before God that Jesus recommends.

All Saints' Day

Sunday between 30 October and 5 November inclusive

Thought for the day

In Christ we are chosen to be God's holy people.

Reflection on the readings

Daniel 7:1-3, 15-18; Psalm 149
Ephesians 1:11-23; Luke 6:20-31

There are occasions when you are caving of suddenly finding yourself in huge, lofty underground caverns with the most beautiful rock formations and colours that take your breath away. And you realise that there would be no easy way of seeing these wonders; the tight and terrifying passages you have just squeezed through are an essential part of the experience.

Perhaps this is a little like the pattern of our spiritual experience, too. We are all chosen in Christ to be saints, and part of the glorious life awaiting God's chosen ones in heaven is the challenging and often uncomfortable journey towards it. You cannot have one without the other, and the expectation of that promised, but unimaginable destination can actually make us happy to be spiritually crawling through mud, or holding our breath through sumps.

Nearly all of us share the forgotten but impressive experience of birth through a narrow and uncomfortable tunnel out into the breadth and light of this world, and many mothers find that the pain of the birthing process is different from other pain because of being positive and full of hope. They are in no way denying the pain, but seeing it (at least with hindsight!) in a wider context.

It is in the wider context of eternity that the Beatitudes make sense, and that our attitude to earthly pressures and persecution lightens. Even these times catch the light of God's love and glory, and so become not just possible to bear but reasons for rejoicing, as they mark out and confirm our route.

As we celebrate today the many who have persevered on this route and now cheer us on, we catch the excitement again of our calling, both individually by name, and as the entire Church of God.

Fourth Sunday before Advent

*Sunday between 30 October and 5 November inclusive**

** For use if the Feast of All Saints was celebrated on 1 November and alternative propers are needed.*

Thought for the day

Jesus came to search out the lost and save them.
Through him we come to our senses
and make our lives clean.

Reflection on the readings

Isaiah 1:10-18; Psalm 32:1-7
2 Thessalonians 1:1-12; Luke 19:1-10

With all the hurt of a parent who expects honesty from a child he loves and finds instead that he is living a lie, God's indignation burns. Perhaps we too have felt the pain of discovering that someone, who has been speaking pleasantly to our faces, has been ridiculing or insulting us behind our backs. The deceit hurts as much as the actual offence.

God cannot bear hypocrisy. All through the Bible, both in the Old and the New Testament, we find this loathing of falsehood and pretence; we get the impression that he would prefer an honest sinner any day to the mealy-mouthed obsequiousness described so well in Dickens' Uriah Heap. In Jesus' day it was the hypocrisy of the Pharisees which most often drew his harshest words.

The Isaiah passage for today makes it quite clear that no efficient worship or complex rituals of sacrifice will ever be acceptable unless they are matched by pure and honourable lives and the awareness of sin. Our worship must simply express the outpouring of our love for God which, as a matter of course, shows itself in our loving behaviour to one another day by day.

Psalm 32 beautifully expresses that wonderful feeling of freedom and lightness that comes when we finally get round to admitting where we are to blame, so that God can at last do something about it and sort us out. Why, we wonder, did we take so long pretending it wasn't a sin!

Perhaps Zacchaeus had spent considerable time and effort persuading himself of all kinds of good reasons for living the life he did, but there was always the deep-down nagging suspicion that there was a better way. Certainly he made quite an effort to see Jesus once he knew he would be in the area, and Jesus, always in touch with his Father's viewpoint, noticed the first tentative reaching out and responded to it.

So it is with us. As soon as we make the first tentative move to desire honesty and cleansed thoughts, God will pick up our longing and run with it, bringing us into contact with help and encouragement or challenge, just as we need it. Real and expensive sacrifices may well need to be made, but we will find we are making them out of choice, without resentment, and over the years God will keep his promise to restore the years the locusts have eaten.

Third Sunday before Advent

Sunday between 6 and 12 November inclusive

Thought for the day

Life after death is not wishful thinking
but a definite reality.

Reflection on the readings

Job 19:23-27a; Psalm 17:1-9
2 Thessalonians 2:1-5, 13-17; Luke 20:27-38

When you have a favourite author, it is disappointing to get to the end of the last available novel she has written; my mother, with considerable enforced reading time, felt quite lost after the Cadfael books ran out. On one occasion I read *War and Peace* straight through twice because I couldn't bear to finish it!

When we set off on the journey of discovery into friendship with God, there is no problem of getting to the end of him, or having to break our relationship with him simply because our physical body has stopped working. We can carry on enjoying his friendship, and an ever-deepening understanding of his nature throughout the whole of eternity. There is no end to God, and, through the redeeming work of Christ, there need be no end to us either, so we can look forward to life beyond death and enjoy the prospect of living in God's company for ever.

The Sadducees had decided that the idea of resurrection wasn't workable and therefore couldn't be true. As so often happens, they were judging God's ways by human limitations. They worked out this complicated problem to make Jesus realise how silly it is to think there can be life after death. Faced with this conundrum he will surely have to admit that they are sensible and right in their belief.

What Jesus does is to show them that they are asking the wrong question. Resurrection life is not a tangled continuation of the earthly order of things, but a new and different experience, just as real but with whole new dimensions of possibility.

It is rather like arguing that caterpillars couldn't possibly fly. In their present state and with their present limitations it is indeed impossible, but the freshly emerging butterfly proves that flying is a perfectly natural progression from leaf munching. Few of us would ever guess that a caterpillar could turn into a butterfly, and similarly we have little exact idea of what our resurrection life will be like. What we do know is that it will be fulfilling and rewarding, full of joy, peace and love.

In the meantime we are to stand firm and stick to the teachings we have been handed down faithfully through the generations in an unbroken line which can be traced back to Christ himself. That will enable us to discern the false rumours from the truth, and we will be ready to enter the glorious heritage of resurrection life in heaven.

Second Sunday before Advent

Sunday between 13 and 19 November inclusive

Thought for the day

There will be dark and dangerous times as the end approaches, but by standing firm through it all we will gain life.

Reflection on the readings

Malachi 4:1-2a; Psalm 98
2 Thessalonians 3:6-13; Luke 21:5-19

The Gospel for today makes terrifying reading. The seemingly solid beauty of the temple seems to have triggered in Jesus a vision of the world from outside time. Like a speeded-up film we scan the great cosmic cycles and seasons, natural disasters and human agonies, as the earth labours towards its time of accomplishment.

Amongst the terror, distress, upheavals and ructions are scattered the bright lights of individuals who are unperturbed and faithful; those who are not drawn into the panic but remain steadfast, strong as rocks in their perseverance.

We may well wonder how we could ever survive; what hope there could possibly be of us joining the number of those who will win eternal life by their endurance. Certainly Jesus is anxious to stress that it will not be an easy ride, nor a natural consequence of setting out with enthusiasm on the Christian journey. We can't take our salvation for granted and then sit back with our feet up.

We are warned of what to expect to enable us to be prepared, and the important truth is that we shall not be doing all this on our own or in our own strength. We will be yoked up with Jesus, sustained by his power and provided with the right words and the necessary courage. Only one second at a time will be expected of us!

There is no way church congregations or individual Christians will be able to shut their doors and hide away from the troubles and threats of the world. Our place is right in the centre of the action, getting involved, and standing up for what is right and just, whatever the personal consequences may be.

Christ the King

Sunday between 20 and 26 November inclusive

Thought for the day

This Jesus, dying by crucifixion between criminals,
is the anointed King of all creation
in whom all things are reconciled.

Reflection on the readings

Jeremiah 23:1-6; Psalm 46
Colossians 1:11-20; Luke 23:33-43

In the passage from Jeremiah we have that wonderful image of God, gathering up all the scattered sheep from where they have bolted in terror and confusion, and bringing them carefully back to their pasture. Good shepherds are appointed to tend them so that they will not be afraid any more. The idea of a Shepherd King touches a deep chord in us; there is a rightness of balance, a wholesome combination of authority and practical caring, which rings true and speaks of safety and security. The tradition is already there in David, the shepherd boy made king, and now it is given even more powerful meaning.

God's great rescue plan is extraordinarily focused at the crossing of two rough pieces of wood, designed for use in Roman executions. Yet it is as if those two pieces of wood, which form the cross on which the Shepherd King hangs dying, extend onwards and outwards across the whole of human experience, the depth of human suffering and the height of human joy. They stretch out to unite our deepest needs with the most complete fulfilment; they draw together all things from all generations and cultures, into that point of reconciliation at the point of complete love.

The cross becomes a throne, where the kingdom of forgiving love is seen in action; costly forgiveness serenaded with insults and sneers. The attendants, finding the innocent Jesus beside them, sharing their hours of deserved agony, are representative of us all. Wherever our wanderings have taken us we need only turn our head to see him there suffering with us. We too can react either in disgust at this terrible vulnerability of God's love, or we can allow the acceptance and forgiveness to work its healing in us, long before we can understand the full implications.

Today we look back over the unfolded story of God's redeeming love that we have explored during the past year, and the journey brings us firmly back to the cross, which fixes and anchors everything. Being a cross, it also points us to look forward, to a deepening understanding of the Incarnation as we approach Advent and Christmas once again.